A prescription for a healthier society, this book describes a proactive approach to creating durable companies intentionally designed to make the world a better place.

—Marc Harrison, MD, President and CEO
of Intermountain Healthcare

An urgent book from one of the world's most forward-thinking venture capitalists. The argument in *Intended Consequences* is built on a searing critique of companies that rush to innovate without consideration of the potentially toxic ripple effects, but the real power in the book comes from its playbook on how to build companies that innovate responsibly, with a more thoughtful, values-driven intentionality. A vital read for any founder committed to building a future-fit business.

—Youngme Moon, Donald K. David Professor of Business
at Harvard Business School and author of *Different*

Hemant makes a powerful case for why companies must own their impact on society. As company builders, we have an opportunity to take on humanity's greatest challenges (climate change, inequality) and to transform vital frontiers (healthcare, energy, finance). Hemant shares a framework for leaders to build intentionally and to create a positive, enduring societal impact. This thesis is the start of a critical global discussion among investors, business leaders, and innovators about how we must harness the power of capitalism and responsible innovation for good above all else.

—Ashwini Zenooz, President and CEO of Commure

Intended Consequences provides invaluable guidance for the emerging data enterprise of the twenty-first century. Taneja and Maney point the way toward a future shaped not by zero-sum trade-offs among stakeholders but by fresh approaches and values-based choices. And while their focus is on startups, the lessons are equally applicable to established enterprises, as we move into a new era of stakeholder capitalism.

—**Jon Iwata,** Executive Fellow at the Yale School of Management and former Chief Brand Officer of IBM

This is a powerful and paradigm-shifting book, which argues—as I firmly believe—that it is not only possible but imperative that today's entrepreneurs and investors do well by doing good in the world. The businesses that will endure and have generation-defining, category-defining impact will do so because they seek to solve real social problems, align their business models with their intentions, and hold themselves accountable for creating lasting outcomes.

—**Toyin Ajayi,** cofounder and President of Cityblock Health

Throughout my career, I've had the privilege of working in innovative environments focused on making a difference. Responsible innovation matters and is foundational in the era of stakeholder capitalism. *Intended Consequences* not only thoughtfully articulates why responsible innovation matters but also provides a framework and actionable plan to incorporate it into the nucleus of a company.

—**Robin Washington,** healthcare entrepreneur and former Chief Financial Officer of Gilead Sciences

UNINTENDED
CONSEQUENCES

UNINTENDED CONSEQUENCES

CONSEQUENCES

HOW TO BUILD
MARKET-LEADING COMPANIES
WITH RESPONSIBLE INNOVATION

HEMANT TANEJA
WITH KEVIN MANEY

New York   Chicago   San Francisco   Athens   London   Madrid
Mexico City   Milan   New Delhi   Singapore   Sydney   Toronto

1 2 3 4 5 6 7 8 9   LCR   26 25 24 23 22 21

ISBN   978-1-264-28549-5
MHID   1-264-28549-3

e-ISBN   978-1-264-28550-1
e-MHID   1-264-28550-7

Library of Congress Cataloging-in-Publication Data

Names: Taneja, Hemant, author. | Maney, Kevin, author.
Title: Intended consequences : how to build market-leading companies
   with responsible innovation / Hemant Taneja with Kevin Maney.
Description: New York : McGraw Hill, [2021] | Includes bibliographical
   references and index.
Identifiers: LCCN 2021038688 (print) | LCCN 2021038689 (ebook) |
   ISBN 9781264285495 (hardback) | ISBN 9781264285501 (ebook)
Subjects: LCSH: Social responsibility of business. | Industries—Social
   aspects. | Disruptive technologies—Social aspects.
Classification: LCC HD60 .T358 2021 (print) | LCC HD60 (ebook) |
   DDC 658.4/08—dc23
LC record available at https://lccn.loc.gov/2021038688
LC ebook record available at https://lccn.loc.gov/2021038689

McGraw Hill books are available at special quantity discounts to use as premiums and sales promotions or for use in corporate training programs. To contact a representative, please visit the Contact Us pages at www.mhprofessional.com.

To all our founders—
who have shown us the extraordinary impact
of building responsibly

CONTENTS

FOREWORD by Kenneth I. Chenault   ix

PART I
The Business Case for Responsible Innovation

CHAPTER 1   The End of Unintended Consequences   3

CHAPTER 2   Principles and Practices of
Responsible Innovation   21

PART II
Mindset: Principles of Responsible Innovation

CHAPTER 3   Innovate for Systemic Change   39

CHAPTER 4   Innovate for Individual Impact   49

CHAPTER 5   Fight Inequality   61

CHAPTER 6   Take Responsibility for Climate Change   73

PART III
Mechanism: Playbook for Building
Responsible Innovation Companies

CHAPTER 7   Responsible Business Models   87

CHAPTER 8   Algorithmic Canaries   103

CHAPTER 9   Ethical Growth   113

CHAPTER 10   Culture and Governance   121

CHAPTER 11 **Stewardship and Antitrust** 131

CHAPTER 12 **Policy Partnerships** 145

EPILOGUE: Questions for Companies 155

ACKNOWLEDGMENTS 163

NOTES 165

INDEX 175

FOREWORD

by Kenneth I. Chenault

In 2018, I joined the venture capital firm General Catalyst upon my retirement as chairman and CEO of American Express, a position I held for 17 years. Many thought my move into venture capital to be an odd choice, but to me, it was an easy decision to join an industry that fuels—and is fueled by—innovation, and to join a mission-driven firm led by people I've known and trusted for many years.

I led American Express for nearly two decades. The company has endured for more than 150 years through financial crises, fierce competition, world wars, and global societal challenges. That gave me a unique perspective on what it takes to create innovative, industry-leading companies built to withstand the test of time. Further, I have always viewed technology as an enabler. I led the digital transformation of American Express and, as part of that work, I spent a great deal of time in Silicon Valley, eventually establishing American Express Ventures.

So, without hesitation, I entered the venture capital industry as the chairman and a managing director of General Catalyst. As an investor, I mentor founders who are building companies well positioned for global scale and for which I believe my leadership experience can positively influence their growth trajectory, business outcomes, and societal impact as they grow to become fundamental institutions. My role at General Catalyst provides me with strong insight into emerging next-generation companies. These companies simultaneously have the incredible opportunity to create businesses that are aligned with the long-term interests of society from the very start, yet they also have the potential to cause harmful unintended consequences when technology is built without forethought or accountability. That perspective, shared by my partners at General Catalyst, combined with the accelerated pace and scale at which technology was being deployed, led to a firmwide commitment to ensure the businesses we back are built for ambitious growth—absolutely—and with the explicit intent to make lasting positive societal impact.

Through the years, I've had the pleasure of working with General Catalyst's Hemant Taneja. I was struck by his commitment to thinking and leading outside of the box, particularly his thought leadership on the critical need for the tech and VC industries to evolve. In 2013, he published his "unscaled" thesis in an article titled "Economies of Unscale: Why Business Has Never Been Easier for the Little Guy" for *Harvard Business Review.* That was followed by his 2018 book, *Unscaled* (also coauthored with Kevin Maney). Last year, he published a second book, *UnHealthcare: A Manifesto for Health Assurance* (coauthored with Stephen Klasko and Kevin Maney), which laid out not just why—but how—the healthcare industry must evolve from a "sick care" system to a resilient, proactive health assurance system. A system designed to help people stay well, bend the cost curve through innovation, and make quality care more affordable and more accessible to all. Through Hemant's vision and investment leadership, General Catalyst is playing an active role in effecting that important change.

At the core of both *Unscaled* and *UnHealthcare* were the early threads of the responsible innovation thesis: the critical need for companies—in particular, venture-backed technology companies—to be engineered from the outset for growth and good, to serve the needs of a broader array of stakeholders, including employees, customers, and investors, and to align with the long-term interests of society.

Back in 2016, Hemant wrote "Silicon Valley Dreams: What If It All Comes True?" followed by "The Era of 'Move Fast and Break Things' Is Over" in 2019. The former called out the use of artificial intelligence (AI), robotics, and virtual reality (VR) and their potential impact on the future of work. The latter was an indictment against the use of technology for the sake of pure disruption, and made a strong case for company creation through collaboration, intentionality, and forethought, especially preventing the unintended consequences of technology. These two pieces were the seminal framing for Hemant's responsible innovation thesis, detailed in this new book, a powerful and timely articulation of Hemant's thought leadership and the framework he has been formulating over the past several years as an investor and company builder. As we have all witnessed, the global pandemic has only exacerbated the societal challenges and inequities brought about by the unintended consequences of technology, laying bare the need for a new framework, a new mindset, and a new set of standards for deploying technology ethically and building and leading enduring companies.

As I've said for many years, including through my tenure as chairman and CEO of American Express, I strongly believe corporations exist because society allows them to exist. Therefore, companies have an obligation to make a positive impact on the world and on society at large. As venture capitalists, we are in a unique position to both effect and champion positive change. We are company creators and builders, counseling and guiding tech companies as they grow. We are accountable for what we enable and produce. Innovation requires responsibility—to generate returns beyond profits and to recenter technology as a force for good in the world.

I recognize the notion of "innovation for good" is not a new concept. ESG (environmental, social, and governance) has been around for years. However, it is focused on a set of outputs established far into a company's growth and evolution, almost after the fact. Responsible innovation is baked into a company's business model, culture, and leadership standards from the outset—at the very beginning. By nature, with the required forethought and intentionality, responsible innovation becomes a part of a company's very being, its vernacular, its mission, and its identity, accountable for its innovation and aligned with the long-term interests of society.

Responsible innovation will require a major shift in the mindset of companies and the very way the innovation community approaches and values its work. That evolution is long overdue. The role of companies and how they operate have not changed drastically over the past century despite dramatic changes in our society. However, the demands on companies, founders, and leaders to align with a broader array of stakeholders and the interests of society are mounting by the day. Employees, customers, and shareholders are increasingly looking to companies to address economic opportunity and inclusion, environmental sustainability, access and diversity, and customer privacy, safety, and well-being. They are demanding that companies and leaders proactively plan for these areas in their business models and create action plans around them with visible, measurable outcomes. They are holding companies accountable—through their voices, their wallets, and their loyalty.

As I said earlier, I have always viewed technology as an enabler. I also believe that customer-centricity must be core to a company's values. The role of a company is, in large part, to help and protect its customers. Technology needs to be managed and used as a tool to meet customer needs.

In the pages of this book, Hemant has rewritten the playbook for what it means to ethically deploy technology and how to build and lead an enduring company. As 2020 made abundantly clear, the technologies of tomorrow will continue to advance at an accelerated rate with the potential to impact lives profoundly, for better or for worse. Inaction is no longer an option. Responsible innovation is critical to the future of business, the future of technology, and the future of society.

Together with the extended General Catalyst team, I look forward to partnering with leaders, founders, policy makers, and fellow investors to fulfill the promise of responsible innovation and to create truly powerful, positive change that endures.

PART I

The Business Case for Responsible Innovation

CHAPTER 1

THE END OF UNINTENDED CONSEQUENCES

Throughout history, technology has often been great. But now it must also be *good*.

Companies that create technology that does good and avoids harmful, unintended consequences will win in the years to come. Investing for financial returns and for positive impact are no longer two different things. They are now the same thing.

Today's powerful technologies have too much destructive potential. We're already seeing how innovations gone awry can divide societies and wreck the climate. The one-two punch of Moore's law and Metcalfe's law means that new technologies and any problems they create can explode into the world at greater velocity than any time in history. Moore's law describes the phenomenon that has made massive computing power supercheap. Metcalfe's law describes how networks get exponentially more powerful as they grow. So with global networks in the cloud and nearly infinite computing power available to most anyone, an app built by two people in a garage today can, in a flash, impact hundreds of millions of users globally.

It took us almost a century to understand that the internal combustion engine was damaging the climate. It only took about 10 years to see social media's poisonous impact on politics, culture, and individuals. Now, imagine how Moore's law and Metcalfe's law could accelerate the damage done by a biased or rogue artificial intelligence.

At the same time, new companies are reinventing nearly every industry. That dynamic is accelerating, given a turbo boost by a pandemic that made us rethink much about life and work. If change of this magnitude is not handled in a way that brings workforces along and helps communities adjust, it will vastly widen wealth and well-being gaps, further tearing at the social order.

Worrisome as all that is, it creates an opportunity.

More than ever, the world needs—and increasingly demands—technology products and services that improve life on this planet while avoiding harmful unintended consequences. "Responsible innovation" is the way to build the great, mission-driven companies that can deliver such products and services. Companies that practice responsible innovation foresee and avoid harmful unintended consequences, and they ensure that their products and services are beneficial.

Here, the word *responsible* has two meanings. The first is about making sure innovations do no harm, which seems like a no-brainer, yet is something too few companies do. The second meaning is to create innovations that solve society's most challenging problems, whether they be climate change, inequality, or an individual's ability to stay healthy.

While I want to make the world better, I'm also a venture capitalist. I want the best returns. And I believe this is now the path to the best returns. As I'll present in this book, responsible companies will win loyal customers, attract quality investment, and recruit and retain the most-talented employees. Responsible companies will beat companies that "move fast and break things," carelessly disrupting the livelihoods of vast swaths of the population.

Running a company solely to meet quarterly numbers and increase shareholder value—a 1970s-era concept championed by economist Milton Friedman—is over. In this new era, impact investing will produce lower risks and better returns. The responsible innovation entrepreneur must be empathetic, understanding deeply the needs of customers and finding a beneficial way to serve them.

Large corporations have for some time embraced the notion of corporate social responsibility (although it can often feel more like a "greenwashing" PR exercise). Today's startups need to embrace their version of startup social responsibility and ensure it is woven deeply into their fabric.

A lot of founders believe they should get to scale first and then worry about fixing the damage they cause. But that doesn't work. By then, their business model is baked and it's too hard to change. All they can do is tinker at the fringes and hope they don't wind up defending themselves in front of Congress or prosecutors. That's no longer a viable strategy.

The philosophical shift toward taking responsibility for technology's impact is profound and historic. Most creators of technology have not worried much about unintended consequences. Technology, in fact, has almost always been considered neutral. Whether a new technology turned out to be beneficial or damaging just depended on the way it was used. The automobile gave us a new freedom of movement, greatly benefiting societies globally. No one in 1900 could have predicted that by 2021 people would own 1.4 billion cars all over the world, and that technology's most terrible unintended consequence now has become apparent: climate change. There's a famous story about IBM's tabulating machines in the 1940s. For two decades, they helped companies organize data, railroads develop schedules, and the Social Security Administration calculate and send out its checks. During World War II, Nazi Germany appropriated the IBM machines left behind after fighting broke out, and it used them to efficiently track many of the Jews it herded into concentration camps. High-fructose corn syrup, first marketed in the early 1970s by the Clinton Corn Processing Company, started as a cheaper sweetener but ended up playing a major role in the world's obesity epidemic. Regulators approved OxyContin because it was found to be safe and effective for pain relief, and then it fueled a devastating addiction problem.

Today, we've become very aware of the rapid acceleration of technology's unintended consequences. Facebook, created to help friends and family stay in touch, has been appropriated to foment political unrest and splinter societies. Millions of consumers love the efficiency of shopping on Amazon.com, but the company is destroying retail stores and, as a result, many jobs and communities. YouTube has been commandeered to spread hate and Twitter to spread fake news. A lot of people believe the world is falling apart because of technology.

Too many companies ignore the unintended (and destructive) consequences of their actions. American sociologist Robert Merton, writing in the 1930s, identified different types of unintended consequences.[1] The first two—the most common—were from *ignorance* and *error*. In other words, the technology took a turn its creators neither intended nor foresaw, and perhaps could not control. But a third, more malicious kind of unintended consequence Merton labeled *imperious immediacy of interest*. It means that a technology's creator allows an unintended harmful effect because it serves the person or company well in the short term. Today's poster child for imperious immediacy of interest is Facebook. But you could also indict oil companies, tobacco companies, soft drink makers, and creators of addictive apps.

Allowing or ignoring unintended consequences for profit is immoral. And because our new technologies are so powerful, society can't afford dangerous consequences caused by ignorance or error. We have to build good technology, understand how it might go bad, and put in place measurements and mechanisms so we can detect and stop harmful consequences before they cause too much damage.

A lot of technology has, of course, done enormous good. It gives us the means to feed 7.8 billion people, extends life spans, spreads knowledge, and gives us indispensable tools like smartphones, laptops, and GPS. During the COVID-19 pandemic, technology brought us a vaccine in record time and allowed the economy to keep going despite a lockdown. It's time to make sure capitalism gets behind more of the good things, and puts an end to the bad.

The Friedman philosophy that companies exist only to increase shareholder value is already dying. I want to bury it. I believe the most successful companies from now on will exist to increase the quality of life on this planet.

––––––––––

For the past decade, I've seen the world through a lens I call "unscaling." I wrote a book about it (also with Kevin Maney, coauthor of this book), titled *Unscaled*.[2]

For most of the twentieth century, the path to business success was economies of scale. Technologies of that era, such as cars and trucks, television, electricity, the telephone, and those IBM tabulating machines, made it possible to scale an enormous company and gave rise to mass media, mass markets, and mass production. The best businesses were those that could scale up to make the most of the same thing for the most people.

But around the mid-2000s, we started creating technologies that could turn that trend on its head: the smartphone, cloud computing, internet-of-things devices, big data, artificial intelligence (AI). It became increasingly possible to use technology to understand, find, and serve small niches of consumers or even individual consumers, and deliver products and services that seem to be built specifically for them. Most people would prefer a bespoke, customized product to a mass-produced one, so unscaled products tend to win versus old mass-market products if the price is right. What's unfolding now is the opposite of mass markets and mass production and the opposite of economies of scale. It's economies of unscale.

This dynamic has been tearing down older, scaled industries and reinventing them. Look at media: network TV aimed at the masses is getting replaced by streaming services that serve up what you want to watch based on your viewing habits. Or education: factory-like schools are being challenged by smart online courses like those from Khan Academy. In healthcare, mass-market medicine is being supplemented by cloud-based services that get to know your health and tailor care to you.

At my firm, General Catalyst, I made unscaling my investment thesis. We've looked for companies that can unscale some part of a major industry—companies such as Livongo Health, Airbnb, Ro, Stripe, Guild Education, Gusto, and Cityblock. These and other companies are building unscaled products that can do enormous good: keep us healthier, reduce carbon emissions, educate our kids better. Still, as I've watched unscaling cascade through industries, I've become concerned. Unscaling's disruption of the economy, when done crudely, can cost people their jobs and hurt communities. The technologies we are developing are so transformative they could make divisions in society much worse than they already are.

Medical technologies driven by AI, robotics, genomics, and gene editing have the potential to open up a biological divide in which the rich get healthier, stronger, and smarter while the poor get left further and further behind. Such potential unintended consequences loom large. They could yield a society we don't want to live in.

AI in particular needs to be checked. When humans build an AI, they can't help but inject their biases. Then, when the AI is unleashed on the world, it exponentially exacerbates those biases. For example, we've seen plenty of stories about how the AI behind facial recognition technology often misidentifies Black people. Such biases can have terrible consequences, as seen in one 2019 shoplifting case in Woodbridge, New Jersey. A store employee called police, and the suspect fled, clipping a police car as he sped away. This was caught on camera, and facial recognition technology identified the man as Nijeer Parks. But he had never even been to Woodbridge. Parks was arrested and spent 10 days in jail before the charges were dismissed. As facial recognition spreads, dangerous mistakes like that will multiply.

There's also widespread concern about AI eating jobs. It's accepted now that AI will lead to autonomous cars and trucks, leaving millions of truck, limo, and bus drivers out of work. That alone will be a monumental challenge for society. But then add to it all the research being done around human longevity. It's likely that some company will come up with an affordable gene therapy that lets everyone live 20 years longer. That means millions of people living longer with no work. That's a recipe for revolution.

The potential for trouble just keeps growing. We're already seeing how AI can be used to create "deep fakes"—videos that look real but aren't. As a warning, a British broadcaster in 2020 made a deep fake of Queen Elizabeth delivering a holiday message. Few could tell it wasn't the queen. I have no doubt deep fakes will be made of other leaders, making them seem to say things that could move people to dangerous acts. We're also seeing stories of the police and military using armed robots and drones to track and even kill criminals and enemies. Add AI to such weaponry, and biases could lead to deadly attacks on the wrong people.

If all that worries you, consider that we're only in the beginnings of the "AI-maker generation." Tools to create AI will soon become so simple to use that people will build AIs as easily as they now make YouTube videos. The potential for chaos when the world gets filled with amateur AI could be nightmarish.

Finally, I'm concerned about monopoly power. The tech industry has always had superpower companies, like IBM and Microsoft in earlier eras. But we've never seen anything like the power and wealth concentrated in Google, Facebook, Apple, and Amazon. The trend is toward greater concentration of power in fewer companies, and those companies can stifle innovative startups to preserve their power and impose rules and practices that benefit them, even if that causes harm. Today's antitrust laws are mostly concerned with protecting consumers from price gouging, which makes little sense at a time when companies like Google and Facebook offer most of their services for free. Antitrust now must protect innovation and business ecosystems.

I will regret it if I help founders build companies that unscale industries and create advanced technologies, and then make the world worse. I'd rather not find myself in the shoes of Roger McNamee, who invested early in Facebook and befriended Mark Zuckerberg, only to later regret the damage caused by Facebook, leading him to write *Zucked*, an anti-Facebook book.

I don't want to start a philanthropic foundation or "lose money" on impact investing to try to atone for the investing I do for returns. I, along with General Catalyst, want to help create conditions so that impact investing and investing for returns are, in fact, the same. This is a journey our firm has been on for two decades, investing in climate-change companies, education, and healthcare. There are huge opportunities in tackling society's big problems.

Why is this not fanciful thinking?

First of all, it's increasingly clear that being irresponsible is high risk. Irresponsible companies get punished—by regulators, consumers, customers, and even their own employees. Regulators and policy makers are coming for rapacious tech companies. European Union regulators have already fined Google and Facebook billions of dollars for privacy breaches and anticompetitive practices. In early 2021, after President Trump used Twitter and Facebook to inflame the protestors who stormed the US Capitol, several members of Congress pledged to take action against irresponsible social media giants. "They bear major responsibility for ignoring repeated red flags and demands for fixes," Sen. Richard Blumenthal, a Democrat from Connecticut, told the *Washington Post.* "They have done enduring damage to their own credibility, and these events will renew and refocus the need for Congress to reform big tech."[3] By mid-2021, Congress was debating six bills designed to do just that. Rep. Jerrold Nadler of New York told the *New York Times* that the bills "pave the way for a stronger economy and a stronger democracy for the American people by reining in anticompetitive abuses of the most dominant firms."[4]

The legal and policy backlash against irresponsible tech keeps building. In 2020, the US Securities and Exchange Commission fined Robinhood Financial $65 million for turning stock trading into an addictive game, which led to many users getting into severe financial distress. In 2021, the company was fined another $70 million by the Financial Industry Regulatory Authority—the largest fine the self-regulating body ever imposed. When Zenefits, founded to help small businesses manage employee benefits such as health insurance, tried to irresponsibly hyperscale, employees ignored mistakes and took shortcuts to keep the growth going, running afoul of state insurance and financial regulators. The company got fined by state after state, and started to buckle. Valued in 2015 at $4.5 billion, Zenefits' valuation got cut in half in a year.

Some of these companies face internal rebellion. In 2020, hundreds of employees at Google's parent, Alphabet, organized into a union, unhappy with management's insensitivity to minorities and women as well as its role in propagating hate speech (Alphabet owns YouTube) and dividing the nation (e.g., biased search results). Parul Koul and Chewy Shaw, who are, respectively, the executive chair and the vice chair of the Alphabet Workers Union, wrote in the *New York Times*: "When Google went public in 2004, it said it would be a company that 'does good things for the world even if we forgo some short-term gains.' Its motto used to be 'Don't be evil.' Alphabet is a powerful company, responsible for vast swaths of the internet. It has a responsibility to prioritize the public good. It has a responsibility to its thousands of workers and billions of users to make the world a better place."[5]

Facebook is dealing with similar internal rumblings and falling morale. An internal survey obtained by the *New York Times* found that in late 2020 only half of Facebook employees felt the company was having a positive impact, down from three-quarters earlier in the year.

It's become obvious that companies that are not responsible innovators risk getting a reputation that makes it harder for them to recruit and retain talent.

As these tech giants stumble, a new generation of company founders is determined to build responsible companies. In her book *Reimagining Capitalism in a World on Fire*, Harvard professor Rebecca Henderson says she saw the hunger for this firsthand: "When I first launched the MBA course that became *Reimagining Capitalism*, there were twenty-eight students in the room. Now there are nearly three hundred, a little less than a third of the Harvard Business School class."[6]

Study after study shows that consumers intend to buy from responsible companies and reject those that cause harm. Research by the NYU Stern Center for Sustainable Business found that sales of "sustainable" consumer products from 2013 to 2018 grew 5.6 times faster than those that were not seen that way.[7] A study by market intelligence firm Mintel found that 35 percent of consumers stopped buying from a brand they perceived as unethical.[8]

Many of the world's biggest investors see these trends and believe they will impact the valuation of companies. "Society is demanding that companies, both public and private, serve a social purpose," wrote Larry Fink, CEO of BlackRock, the world's largest financial asset manager, in a letter to CEOs of companies in the firm's portfolio. "To prosper over time, every company must not only deliver financial performance, but also show how it makes a positive contribution to society. Companies must benefit all of their stakeholders, including shareholders, employees, customers, and the communities in which they operate."[9]

You can already see what could happen to companies that ignore such entreaties by looking at ExxonMobil. In 2021, the company was stunned by a revolt by shareholders who wanted to force it to transition from an oil and gas company into a responsible energy company. This came after investors pounded the company for its climate-damaging operations. In 2013, ExxonMobil was the biggest company in the United States. Then, as *New York Times* columnist Thomas Friedman wrote: "As a result of its head-in-the-oil-sands-drill-baby-drill-we-are-still-not-at-peak-oil business model, Exxon lost over $20 billion last year, suffered a credit rating downgrade, might have to borrow billions just to pay its dividend, has seen its share price over the last decade produce a minus-30 percent return and was booted from the Dow Jones industrial average."[10]

We're seeing movement toward responsible innovation all over the world. In 2019, the Business Roundtable, which includes CEOs of many of the biggest US companies, released a groundbreaking statement kicking Friedman's shareholder-first dogma in the teeth by declaring that the purpose of a corporation is now "to promote an economy that serves all Americans." In 2020, the Vatican, along with businesses and investors that represent $2.1 trillion in market cap, created the Council for Inclusive Capitalism. Pope Francis made a statement about the new group: "An economic system that is fair, trustworthy and capable of addressing the most profound challenges facing humanity and our planet is urgently needed." In the United Kingdom, Cambridge University launched the first master's degree in responsible AI. "It's crucial that future leaders are trained to manage [AI's] risks so we can make the most of this amazing technology," said Stephen Cave, the program's executive director. (I teach a course at Stanford that encourages engineers to think this way.) Italy, Japan, Singapore, the United Arab Emirates, and the United Kingdom signed on to a program they're calling the Agile Nations Charter, with a "mission to make it easier for businesses within their jurisdictions to introduce and scale innovations across their markets while upholding protections for citizens and the environment."[11]

In short, responsible innovation and curtailing unintended consequences are going to be an important global conversation this decade. Every part of the business ecosystem is seeing that we will destroy our future if we don't change.

You can see the future coming. Responsible innovation companies are not mythical entities. They exist. No one company excels in every dimension, and everyone's definition of a "responsible" company might be different. But I know of many companies shining a light in the direction we need to go.

Tesla may be the most successful company practicing responsible innovation, at least in regard to climate change.

CEO Elon Musk set out to build a company that would directly address the problem of carbon emissions.[12] To do that, he built the world's first widely desired electric car. To make a popular electric car, he had to develop new battery technology, which turns out to be critical to building out the solar energy industry since it addresses the need for energy when the sun isn't shining. To complete the circle, Tesla now makes a Solar Roof that can take the place of a typical roof and generate solar power, which can then be stored in Tesla batteries. (The company is also developing AI for self-driving cars and trucks, which could present challenges when it comes to unintended consequences.) As of this writing, Tesla's market cap is around $650 billion, more than eight times the market cap of General Motors, and it has forced the global auto industry to get serious about electric cars. In Tesla's case, creating good technology has paid off enormously well. (For Musk, too, as his net worth in January 2020 was around $167 billion.)

There are also Fortune 500 companies I would call enduring responsible companies. They've operated for decades with a broader mission than just increasing shareholder value.

Pharmaceutical giant Merck always believed scientific discovery was the key to its business success and its impact on global health. While most major pharma companies over the past two decades cut their research and development (R&D) and became marketers of products engineered by startups, Merck continues to spend about 22 percent of its revenue on R&D. By late 2020, it had treatments for HIV, heart failure, and melanoma in late-stage trials.

Consumer products company Unilever always seems to look for ways to make products sustainable. Paul Polman, who retired in 2019 after a decade as CEO, told a journalist: "I discovered a long time ago that if I focus on doing the right thing for the long term to improve the lives of consumers and customers all over the world, the business results will come."

And a new generation of responsible innovation companies are emerging. General Catalyst has funded some. Gusto is a cloud service that helps small businesses manage payroll and benefits, with a mission of making it easier for anyone to start and run a company. Spring Discovery is working on ways to slow aging and keep people healthier longer. It is dedicated to serving all of society, not just the wealthy. Cityblock has built a vibrant business by bringing better healthcare to populations, such as the homeless, that typically get terrible healthcare. All operate in accordance with responsible innovation principles and seek to foresee and avoid unintended consequences—and all are building solid, fast-growing, valuable businesses. (More on those companies in later chapters.)

Livongo is a company I cofounded with healthcare industry veteran Glen Tullman. Our goal was to improve the experience of people with chronic health conditions such as diabetes. The old healthcare system treats everyone with diabetes the same, even though every diabetic experiences the disease differently. So we used AI to learn about each user's diabetes and help them manage it so they stay out of the doctor's offices and hospitals. Unlike Facebook or Twitter, our goal was *disengagement*, not engagement. Livongo serves customers better and has a better business if we help people so they can use the product less. In 2020, Teledoc bought Livongo for $18.5 billion. I'm proud to say that I've experienced success with responsible innovation and believe in it.

Until recently, it was believed that doing "good" and battling harmful consequences meant sacrificing growth and profits while less responsible companies flourished. But as these and other companies are proving, new tools and management practices are making it possible to anticipate unintended consequences before they become dangerous and build business models that do better.

This is profoundly important because I believe capitalism is a huge enabler of positive change if directed in the right ways. Tesla set an example. We've seen decades of policies and regulations aimed at protecting the environment, but this company's success moved the whole auto industry toward sustainability. Livongo and companies like it are altering the broken US healthcare system in ways policy makers never could. If we get capitalism aligned behind the changes we seek as a society, we will course-correct faster than any other way.

In that sense, Friedman is helpful when it comes to defining the purpose of a company. His famous 1970 essay railed against business leaders getting involved in the social and political issues of the 1960s—running the business on one hand, but thinking they have a "social responsibility" to spend resources on other issues. Social issues should be up to individuals, he argued, not companies. So he concluded that a company's responsibility is only to increase profits and shareholder value.

But now the most profitable and valuable businesses will be those built to improve society. "Business" and "social responsibility" are no longer two different things. Which, in a weird way, makes Friedman right. If a business model based on social good makes more profits and creates more value, then the mantra that a company's job is to increase profits and value align. In fact, the more profits, the more good the business will do.

That is the essence of new business models built for responsible innovation.

CHAPTER 2

PRINCIPLES AND PRACTICES OF RESPONSIBLE INNOVATION

In the previous chapter, I argued the most successful companies over the next couple of decades will be those that practice responsible innovation. They will seek to build technology that benefits all stakeholders, and they'll try to foresee and avoid harmful unintended consequences.

But how? Doing all that requires thinking in ways that refute Silicon Valley's conventional wisdom. *Move fast, break things, and hope for the best* won't work anymore. Nor will recklessly releasing *minimum viable products* and hoping they don't do any damage—companies instead must think in terms of *minimum virtuous products*. Other tech industry practices that have become problematic include the drive for hyperscale, a winner-take-all mentality, and prioritizing shareholder value above all other outcomes.

There are two fundamental pillars to building a responsible innovation company in the 2020s:

- **Pillar 1: Mindset.** Paramount when setting your company's mindset is a simple idea: plan to endure. Your motivation should be to create positive consequences and solve important problems over the long haul—so your company will endure for a long time. That idea alone will prod company leaders to think through what problems they might solve for the world, the culture they'll want to develop, and how things could go wrong.

- **Pillar 2: Mechanism.** A proper company mindset alone isn't enough: you need mechanisms that make sure the mindset gets supported. Build a business model that rewards positive consequences and discourages unintended consequences. Embrace a set of key consequence indicators (KCIs)—more on that in a bit—that tell you if you're on the right track. Such mechanisms have been missing from almost every other call for stakeholder capitalism, conscious capitalism, social responsibility, and so on. All of those rely almost entirely on good intentions. But the only way to make sure that responsible innovation endures is to align financial and business model incentives with intentions. Otherwise, a company will eventually be forced to make a devil's choice between the two, and in market capitalism, financial results almost always trump good intentions.

Mindset and *mechanism* must synchronize and support each other—a responsible innovation company's yin and yang. The best intentions get nowhere without the mechanisms to make them happen. The best mechanisms won't matter if the mindset is shallow or the culture is toxic.

To start down the path of responsible innovation a company must make those two pillars a priority. The leadership team should continuously ask relevant questions like: What do we have to do to endure for decades? Once we set our business model and product in motion, what could go wrong? What kind of culture must we create so that coming generations follow through on good intentions?

A few years ago, Airbnb CEO Brian Chesky realized it was time for the company to have that kind of conversation—10 years after he founded Airbnb with Joe Gebbia and Nathan Blecharczyk. Chesky said he wanted to institutionalize the founders' intentions. The timing was right: "We are now big enough where anything is possible, but not so big that change would be nearly insurmountable," he wrote at the time.

The result was a remarkable document published in January 2018: "An Open Letter to the Airbnb Community About Building a 21st Century Company." In it, Chesky laid out his vision for enduring responsible innovation. "It's clear our responsibility isn't just to our employees, our shareholders, or even to our community—it's also to the next generation. Companies have a responsibility to improve society, and the problems Airbnb can have a role in solving are so vast that we need to operate on a longer time horizon."[1] In fact, he teed up an "infinite time horizon" for Airbnb, and by thinking in those terms, "a company can be more audacious, take more responsibility for what they make, and create more lasting change."

The time horizon would pair with Airbnb's other big goal: serving all stakeholders, which Chesky listed as employees, shareholders, guests, hosts, and the world outside Airbnb. "To be a 21st-century company, we must find harmony between these stakeholders." (As part of its responsible innovation effort, Airbnb brought in as a board member Ken Chenault— my mentor and author of this book's Foreword, a partner at General Catalyst, and former CEO of American Express.)

Two years later, in January 2020, Chesky followed up by putting some incentives behind his intentions.[2] In a document titled "An Update on Our Work to Serve All Stakeholders," he published metrics that would help the company track its success in meeting its intentions. The metrics were then tied to compensation for management and employees. He ended by promising, "We are nowhere near finished. This is our first, simple update."

With both of those documents, and in Chesky's everyday management of Airbnb, he is taking the most important steps toward building an enduring responsible company: setting his sights on a long time horizon and influencing Airbnb's culture so it fosters a belief in making sure the product and company do good.

While it may be easier for a startup or decade-old company to set a course for responsible innovation, it's certainly possible for a company of any age or stature to do so—as Fortune 500 glass company Corning has shown. By 2000, Corning had been around for nearly 150 years. It was behind many of the world's breakthrough glass products, from the glass for Thomas Edison's lightbulb to the first TV tubes, Pyrex lab glass, and those Corningware dishes your grandparents might have owned. These days Corning makes the glass on just about every smartphone and flat-screen TV.

The company also invented fiber optics in 1970, and over the following decades became the world leader in that field. During the telecom and dot-com boom of the late 1990s, Corning's fortunes and stock price rocketed. Demand for fiber, analyst firms declared, would be overwhelming far into the future. As a lot of companies might, Corning saw this and went all in, betting almost everything on fiber while some of its other businesses declined. It abandoned many of its good intentions, including its devotion to R&D, to bet big on what was hot.

When the dot-com and telecom boom crashed in 2000, that eviscerated demand for fiber and, in the process, nearly killed Corning. From late 2000 to 2002, the company's stock dove from more than $100 a share to less than $2.

In response, then CEO Jamie Houghton and then COO Wendell Weeks laid off half of all employees and stabilized the company. Then they held a series of meetings to decide what Corning should be. The remarkable first-order conclusion they came to: Corning had already been an important, successful company for 150 years, so it had to be an important, successful company for 150 more.[3]

Imagine starting with a 150-year commitment. A cascade of decisions naturally followed. First, management had to rebuild a foundation for the company on the one thing it was best in the world at doing: difficult material science innovation. But material science starts in research labs and takes a long time, so the company would have to manage long product cycles. To do that effectively, management would need to cultivate long-term buy-in from all its stakeholders. Corning would need customers who share Corning's vision, investors who see beyond the next quarter, and patient partners and suppliers.

The outcome: Corning put in place a strategic framework that discourages it from chasing a single business for the sake of profits and shareholder value; instead, it guides the leadership team to invest in hard innovation that makes the world better and benefits all its stakeholders. (In the 1990s, Corning was spending as little as 4 percent of revenues on R&D. Now it's more than 10 percent.) Weeks became CEO in 2005 and has led a long, steady period of responsible growth. By 2021, Corning had about $12 billion in annual revenue, 50,000 employees, and a stock price of around $41.

I'm not saying Corning is a perfect example of a responsible innovation corporation, but it is a great example of how planning to endure can positively impact a company's direction, values, incentives, and success.

Corning made that shift 150-plus years into its existence, but for some companies there comes a point when it's too late to change. Facebook and Google have enormously profitable business models based on advertising. The platforms are so attractive to advertisers because Google and Facebook collect data about their users that allow ads to be precisely targeted. That creates a financial incentive for Google and Facebook to encroach on our privacy and learn as much about us as they can, so the ad targeting can be ever more effective. On top of that incentive, the more that people engage with Google and Facebook, the more opportunities the companies have to serve us ads and make more money. That creates a financial incentive to drive engagement—to keep people glued to their screens. What makes people engage more? Content that makes them emotional, like extremist political videos and messages.

All of this adds up to a pile of financial incentives that encourage bad behavior: invading privacy, serving up extreme content and fake news, driving engagement to unhealthy levels. Mark Zuckerberg at Facebook and Sundar Pichai, CEO of Google's parent, Alphabet, can strenuously profess good intentions, but their incentives pull too strongly in the other direction. These companies are so profitable, they can't unhook themselves from their faulty business models without collapsing their businesses. Both companies' leaders are backed into a corner.

Maybe if Google or Facebook had a near-death experience, they'd recalibrate and change. But that doesn't seem likely.

———

While some of the old tenets that used to drive the tech industry need to be thrown out or rethought, the industry also needs new tenets for an era of responsible innovation and the end of unintended consequences. What follows are some to consider.

MEASURE WHAT *REALLY* MATTERS

It's hard to manage or improve what you can't measure, and it's important to measure the right things. For the past couple of decades, the tech industry has focused on certain key performance indicators (KPIs) that include metrics like user growth, engagement, retention, revenue, and burn rate. These metrics focus on *how* the product or company is doing. I believe management should focus more on *what* the product or company is doing—particularly what it's doing to (and for) users, stakeholders, and society.

Instead of KPIs, we need KCIs—key consequence indicators. There are no business-school standard KCIs, but some responsible companies have been creating their own and using them as measuring sticks. I've already mentioned Airbnb. Another example is biotech company Vertex Pharmaceuticals, founded in 1989 in Boston. On the company's website, you'll find a page labeled "Key Corporate Responsibility Metrics," and under that: "We are committed to responsible business practices, and measure our progress and impacts."[4] Some of the metrics include the percentage of employees who volunteer in the community, diversity of the leadership team, R&D investment as a percentage of business operating expenses, and emissions and garbage produced. Some of Vertex's metrics, like volunteer participation, miss the mark on measuring the impact of its products, but it's going in the right direction. The best sets of KCIs will focus on measuring a company's external impact.

Another approach gaining momentum is the use of ESG metrics—environmental, social, and governance. It's a start, but those, too, are not standardized and in many cases not effective at showing the impact of a product or company. "Our current focus on ESG measurement is dangerously narrow," wrote Jennifer Howard-Grenville, professor at Cambridge Judge Business School in England, in early 2021. "It fails to capture the complex, systemic nature of social and environmental systems, and indeed that of business organizations themselves."[5] The business world clearly needs innovation around how to measure the consequences of products and companies.

STRIVE FOR DISENGAGEMENT

For the past two-plus decades, consumer technology has constantly vied for a greater share of our attention, trying to keep us riveted to YouTube, Instagram, LinkedIn, or Angry Birds. There wasn't much thought about whether all that attention paid was making anyone's life better or creating a better community. In many cases, such attention-sucking can be damaging, eating up time that might be spent with friends or doing productive work. Nevertheless, engagement long remained the goal—that was what drew advertisers or kept subscribers paying.

The best companies now strive for disengagement. Think of it this way: if a product is intended to help you accomplish something in real life, then the goal should be for the product to do it efficiently and quickly, so you have to use the product less.

Livongo made me a believer in disengagement. We started with the realization that people who have diabetes want to think about their condition as little as possible and get on with the rest of their lives. So we built a cloud service that would help each individual learn how to manage his or her diabetes so well they would rarely have to go to a hospital or doctor's office, and would have to use our technology less. We don't get paid to have people engage with our app, we get paid to help them live better—and spend less money on healthcare.

RELY ON INTENTIONALITY, NOT SERENDIPITY

Most technology companies don't spend a lot of time thinking about consequences. Look at the language they have used for a generation. "Move fast and break things" may be the ultimate "Who cares?" statement. "Minimum viable product" means putting something out into the market the minute it basically works, and then seeing how it gets used or what breaks. Not much thought is given to the damage a half-finished, ill-thought-out product might do. Such companies turn the public into guinea pigs: let's give them this "thing" and see what happens.

Such tactics become dangerous in this era when apps can spread globally in an instant and a rogue AI can destroy people's lives. Instead, companies need intentionality. They must think through a product's impact and guide it with a steady hand. Don't move fast and break things—move appropriately and fix society's problems. Don't put out minimum viable products; make sure they are *minimum virtuous products.*

No one can absolutely know how a product will impact people and society, but it would be an improvement if companies tried to think it through. "It's difficult to know in advance how people will use a new product or all the consequences of a new technology," says Jeff Hawkins, cofounder of Numenta, which is melding brain science and AI research. (Hawkins also created the Palm Pilot in the 1990s.) "We try to anticipate how a product will be used, but it is important to not assume you know, and constantly observe what is actually happening."[6]

SEEK RETURN PLUS IMPACT

Founding or investing in a company that would make the most money was almost always a different goal from founding or investing in a company that would have a positive impact. Today they are the same. In fact, many of the best opportunities for technology companies are in solving some of society's most challenging problems. They include:

Systemic change. Many of society's major systems and institutions are failing or ossifying. Healthcare is a good example. The United States lives with an expensive, bloated system that gives most people a lousy experience and produces mediocre outcomes compared to other countries' health systems. A decade ago, few startups would touch healthcare. The industry seemed almost impossible to break into and make an impact. Now we see a torrent of startups aimed at reinventing different facets of healthcare, all trying to improve both the experience and outcomes. Companies are seeing similar large opportunities to reinvent other creaking systems such as politics, education, and transportation.

Individual impact. Thanks to AI, big data, cloud, mobile, and other forces driving unscaling, cloud services can have a profound impact on individuals. It's now possible for an AI to get to know *you* and help you solve your personal challenges. That's the philosophy behind Livongo. Stitch Fix uses a unique business model and AI to understand a customer's taste in clothing, and sends clothes that fit that taste. A number of new financial technology apps get to know an individual's financial situation and try to help the person improve it. A decade ago, the all-too-true joke went, too many startups focused on replicating what your mother used to do for you—bring you food, do your laundry, pick out your clothes. Today's opportunities are in helping adults overcome challenges and enjoy better, fuller lives.

Inequality and inclusion. Divisions in society seem to get worse every day—giant wealth gaps, health gaps, opportunity gaps. I see two ways companies can succeed by addressing these challenges.

One is to build products or services that directly try to solve inequality and help with inclusion. For instance, Cityblock, which spun out of Google, now has a $1 billion business helping the poorest and sickest people stay healthier and get access to care. A decade ago, few would have thought that could be a good business. Turns out it's a great business. Another example: Boston-based The Predictive Index does psychographic testing to help companies hire, promote, and manage people better. One important element of that is the ability to erase bias from those decisions, which helps chip away at inequality in the workplace.

Companies can also make a difference by minding their own practices. Diversity in hiring is no longer just a nice box to check—it's a key to success in an increasingly diverse world. Nowhere is that more critical than in the development of AI. When building an AI, developers give the algorithms certain goals and train it on data that will help it learn how to achieve those goals. If all the developers are young White males, they will build an AI from the point of view of young White males, giving it biases they may not intend. That's why Google AI scientists made a public demonstration of their unhappiness when management fired Timnit Gebru, a well-known Black AI researcher who forcefully spoke out about the need for more diversity at the company.[7] Her former team wrote a letter to CEO Pichai saying that researching and implementing ways to reduce the harm of AI on marginalized groups is important to their mission. The way to do that is to have people like Gebru on the team.

Climate change. No issue is more important globally than climate change. Creating innovations to help solve it is one of the greatest business opportunities of our generation. Those innovations may be the driving focus of a company, such as at Impossible Foods (meat without animals) or Everlane (a fashion startup that makes clothes from recycled water bottles). Or it could be a dedicated side project, like what Stripe is doing by funding projects that take carbon out of the atmosphere. One project, for instance, is developing a way to embed carbon in concrete that is then used in buildings. On the flip side, companies that exacerbate climate change will be severely punished.

I'll dive deeper into all of these opportunities in the coming chapters.

Many people might be skeptical about responsible innovation, believing it's a lot of PR hot air designed to appease the public and policy makers. That's understandable because that's what it mostly was in years past. But this time it's different—because we have no choice. If companies ignore society's divisions, climate change, and the potential dangers of AI, we'll wind up with an environmental and civil catastrophe.

If you want evidence that companies are finally taking responsible innovation seriously, look at General Motors. In January 2021, CEO Mary Barra boldly announced that by 2035, GM will sell only vehicles that have zero tailpipe emissions, which essentially means electric cars. "General Motors is joining governments and companies around the globe working to establish a safer, greener and better world," Barra said in a statement. "We encourage others to follow suit and make a significant impact on our industry and on the economy as a whole."[8]

I believe the shift to responsible innovation will look something like the quality movement of the 1980s. In the sixties and seventies, many US manufacturers let quality slip. In the absence of much global competition, they found they could pump out low-quality products, which cost less to make, and rake in bigger profits. Then Japanese companies discovered the quality-management concepts preached by American consultant W. Edwards Deming. By the late 1970s, cars from Toyota and Honda were capturing market share from American automakers Ford, GM, and Chrysler. It became clear consumers preferred cars that didn't break down. (One joke in that era was that Ford stood for "fix or repair daily.") Japan also started winning in electronics like TVs and stereos.

US companies that had paid lip service to quality suddenly took it seriously, embracing Total Quality Management and Six Sigma Manufacturing. Deming and other leaders of the quality movement told CEOs that quality is a whole-company exercise, and they emphasized the improvement of products and services over short-term financial goals. Over time, Deming promised, the bet on quality would pay off in happier customers, more efficient operations, improved reputations, *and* a healthier bottom line. He said companies that failed to embrace quality might profit in the short run but would ultimately lose to competitors making higher-quality products.

"Quality used to be a niche," says Nitin Nohria, former dean of Harvard Business School. "That changed in a span of 10 years. In a decade it became associated with good management practices." We're seeing a similar bandwagon effect now around responsible innovation, he says. "The management innovation lies in not seeing it as a trade-off."[9]

Major corporations such as GM and Corning; growing young companies like Airbnb; startups such as Cityblock and Mindstrong—they are all discovering that acting responsibly, solving big problems, and staying mindful of unintended consequences is good business. As they start winning market share from less-responsible competitors, luring the best talent, and getting higher valuations from investors, you can bet that other companies will follow.

PART II

Mindset: Principles of Responsible Innovation

CHAPTER 3

INNOVATE FOR SYSTEMIC CHANGE

Some of the most important and valuable companies of the next 20 years are likely being formed right now. They will succeed because they are being built to solve systemic, societal problems—big problems such as climate change, inequality, divisiveness, disease, hunger, obesity, addiction, and extremism. AI and other technologies developed over the past decade (cloud, mobile, blockchain, genomics) are making it possible to solve such problems in new ways.

That's great for society and for business because the hardest problems are often the most explosive opportunities. Founders who crack those problems will get rewarded much the way Elon Musk is getting rewarded for Tesla's leadership in reducing carbon emissions.

However, there's a danger here. The greater the change, the more chance for serious unintended consequences. Founders and CEOs must appreciate the first-, second-, and third-order possibilities of the transformation they're driving. They have to assume responsibility for the impact of their innovations. Otherwise, good intentions can lead to worse—or different—problems, which can spell disaster for the company.

While I was in the middle of writing this book, Robinhood Financial vividly illustrated the delicate balance between power and responsibility in society-changing innovation. Robinhood's founders, Vlad Tenev and Baiju Bhatt, started their no-fee stock trading platform with what seemed like good intentions for society. They were working in New York City when the Occupy Wall Street movement highlighted the expanding gap between the richest 1 percent and the other 99 percent of the population. "We conceived Robinhood to level that playing field," Tenev wrote on CNBC.com. "We pioneered commission-free trading, enabling millions of underserved people to get more involved in the economy and to make choices to shape their own financial futures. Because of our impact, an entire industry changed—and now most brokerage platforms offer commission-free trading."[1]

All that's true. Robinhood created a simple, gamelike mobile app built to appeal to inexperienced and intimidated investors. Find a stock, click to buy—Robinhood makes it as easy as ordering towels on Amazon. The service charges no fees or commissions, further lowering barriers to individuals who want to trade stocks.

Individual investors liked what Robinhood was doing. By mid-2020, it had 13 million users, heavily skewing under age 30. Its revenue, just $2.9 million in 2015, shot to $180 million in the second quarter of 2020. In early 2021 the company was valued at around $12 billion and made plans to go public. It appeared Robinhood was helping young individuals build wealth, both solving a societal problem and operating a good business.

However, Robinhood makes most of its money through a process called payment for order flow. When an individual trades using the app, Robinhood sends that trade to a larger financial entity, which aggregates orders and places thousands of orders at once. The larger entity then compensates Robinhood for the orders. So, the more orders Robinhood gets—in other words, the more it drives engagement—the more the company makes. Robinhood professes to be solving a problem for its users (access to markets and, ultimately, wealth), but it is doing it through a business model of engagement, not disengagement. That sets up a conflict critics could see early on. "Is it ethical to get people addicted to these bottomless wells [of activity]?" Lex Sokolin, then director of Fintech Strategy at Autonomous Research, told *Fast Company* in 2017. He compared Robinhood to addictive apps like Instagram, adding: "Here, you're not only using people's time, you're also putting their money at risk."[2]

By 2019, regulators were concerned that Robinhood was luring people into playing the market without giving them enough education and protection. One user, just 20 years old, committed suicide after piling up $730,000 in debt from margin trades. Regulators fined the company $65 million in 2020 for its gamification of trading—and another $70 million in 2021. Robinhood's founders may have had good intentions, but they were failing to manage the unintended consequence of people getting into financial trouble because of the app.

And then came the GameStop frenzy of January 2021.

For a few weeks, it was the biggest business story. Members of a Reddit forum called WallStreetBets noticed that institutional and hedge fund short sellers had swarmed the stock of video game retailer GameStop. The WallStreetBets members consider themselves a loose band of swashbuckling financial pirates. They self-organized to thwart the short sellers by buying GameStop stock and driving up the price, so the shorts would lose big and the members would, theoretically, make tons of money.

The group organized their assault on Reddit, and most of the members used Robinhood to make their trades, thanks to its lack of fees, simplicity, and popularity with young traders. Robinhood got overwhelmed with orders. GameStop shares, priced at $35 on January 15, 2020, blasted skyward, peaking at $483.

The volume almost took down Robinhood. It ran out of cash needed to cover the surging volume of trades and had to briefly shut off trading, leaving users who'd bought GameStop unable to get out as the stock dove. Robinhood then had to raise an emergency $3 billion from investors in order to reopen trading. The fiasco nearly broke and definitely embarrassed Robinhood, while raising troubling questions about how easily stocks can be manipulated and the power of hedge funds versus individual investors.

It's hard to say whether Robinhood is helping solve a societal problem or making it worse. Small investors feel empowered by what they witnessed with the GameStop gambit, and policy makers are asking questions that could lead to fairer market regulation. At the same time, Robinhood allowed its users to take enormous, life-altering risks and may have helped prove that hedge funds and institutions will take advantage of individual investors every time. By early February, GameStop shares had fallen back to $90, wiping out many of those who jumped into the frenzy hoping to score big.

Despite all this, Tenev believes he's still on target with his original mission. "What we are witnessing is a massive transformation taking place across financial markets, driven by the intersection of technology, democracy and finance, and one that is ushering in an entirely new era of financial participation and market dynamics," he wrote in *USA Today* in the middle of the GameStop meltdown. "We will stand right beside everyday people in our mission to break down barriers to open the financial system."[3]

But the point remains: It's clear Robinhood never foresaw or thought through the second- and third-order unintended consequences that might result from its product. By tackling social change, Tenev and Bhatt built a company that won boatloads of attention, pulled in a fast-growing user base, and drove the company to a multibillion-dollar valuation. But they also let the consequences of that change get away from them, imperiling everything they had built. How it will turn out is anyone's guess, but it would've turned out better had Robinhood engaged in responsible innovation.

It's hard to think of a bigger problem to solve than aging. Getting old sucks. Diseases related to aging, like Alzheimer's and prostate cancer, are horrendous for the afflicted and colossally costly to treat. Thanks to AI, genomics, and nearly infinite computing power, it's become possible to understand the aging process and, essentially, fix it, or at least fix aspects of it.

But the size of the problem brings with it enormous danger of unintended consequences. What happens to society if many more people live longer and stay healthier? What would happen if wealthy people could slow aging but the rest can't afford that regimen? What happens to innovation if the market is overrun by old people who don't like change?

Spring Discovery is a startup tackling the problem of aging. Its CEO, Ben Kamens, is grappling with the challenge of foreseeing long-term unintended consequences and has set in motion a business model and culture that will, he hopes, help the company steer toward good consequences.

When forming Spring, the first question Kamens had to answer was, why do this at all? A fountain of youth seems like a myth and as imprudent to pursue as a time machine. And even if you could do it, wouldn't you be screwing with the natural order of things in a way that could backfire terribly?

Turns out those first-order questions are the easier ones to answer, as Kamens explains. First, it's not a myth—it's doable. Aging is tied to changes in the body's cells. It's been proven that those cells can be tweaked, and science is on a path to finding out how to tweak them so they age less rapidly, or not at all. So, to Kamens, the first reason to build Spring is to help make sure the technology is *good*. "I'm of the conviction that we can't put the science back in the bottle, so I want to accelerate it and help guide this process," he says.[4]

Does antiaging mess with nature in a dangerous way? Kamens tosses that aside by noting that we've already radically extended life expectancy. Centuries ago, comparatively few people lived past 40; now people regularly live past 80. It's happened gradually as we've learned to treat or cure more diseases that would otherwise kill people. The same is likely to happen with antiaging therapies, but in reverse. If we stop cells from aging as fast, a lot of diseases that happen because of aging will go away or happen later in life, so instead of getting cancer at 70, people will stave off cancer until 80, and eventually until 90. "Suffering caused by disease is a bad thing," Kamens reasons. "It's good to reduce suffering at the hand of science."

All of this shows that Kamens has thought through first-order consequences of Spring's research. It gets harder to see longer-term consequences. But here's the difference between Spring and Robinhood: Spring is looking ahead and asking, what will happen if we're successful?

First, Spring wants its products to be available for everyone, not just the wealthy. "Our business model is built on the presupposition that we're not trying to build something only accessible by the rich," Kamens says. Spring isn't developing a multithreaded spalike treatment plan aimed at keeping someone young forever. It's chasing a small-molecule drug that would permeate all of your cells and slow their aging mechanism. Aging is by definition the most common "disease" on the planet—everyone has it! So the best business plan for Spring is to make something that much of the population can take. "We want to maximize access," Kamens says. "We want governments to pay for this." (No indication so far that they will.)

As for downstream impacts if billions of people live longer, Kamens is optimistic yet thoughtful. "It seems foolish to not make progress in an area like reducing disease because we're afraid we won't make progress in something like increasing the food supply," he says. He wants Spring's culture to encourage awareness of innovations in parallel with aging research, in areas such as food production, housing, economic policy—and the issue of AI eating jobs, possibly leaving much of humanity living longer with nothing to do. "I'm a long-term optimist," Kamens says. "I tend to believe that when it comes to AI replacing jobs, humanity does find the next set of jobs and challenges, even if it's hard to imagine now."

I invested in Spring because I believe it will be a paragon of responsible innovation. The company plans to endure (Kamens, after all, is a long-term optimist), and has a business model (a drug for the masses) that should keep Spring aimed at good consequences. Spring is chasing an enormous opportunity because it's solving an enormous problem. And Kamens is creating a culture that will always pay attention to the consequences of its products. "We want to always be asking, what angles do we take so we don't wake up in 20 years and wonder what we've done?" he says.

———

Emerging technologies make it *possible* to innovate for major societal change. That's a big difference from even a decade ago, and a reason responsible innovation is now so critical.

Previously, I explained the concept of unscaling in Chapter 2. Today's burst of technology innovation is similar to another tech explosion from about 1890 to 1920 that drastically changed our way of living. We're now in a similar 30-year explosion of world-changing technologies. It started around 2007, with smartphones and cloud computing. (Apple introduced the iPhone in 2007; Amazon created Amazon Web

Services in 2006.) In the 2010s, we saw the emergence of truly useful AI (IBM's Watson won on *Jeopardy!* in 2011) and revolutions in genomics (the gene-editing tool CRISPR was invented in 2009). We're also seeing the unfolding of 3D printing, blockchain, and virtual reality.

Those technologies are allowing us to reinvent the world in ways that are different from last century's era of scale and mass markets. Serving niche markets of passionate customers now beats addressing mass markets of merely satisfied customers—because who wouldn't prefer a product or service tailored just for them? We can make autonomous vehicles and rethink transportation; we can do our jobs from anywhere and rethink offices and the nature of work; we can reinvent healthcare so it is more personal, more proactive, and cheaper; we can rethink manufacturing to eliminate waste and reduce carbon emissions. With enormous opportunities like that, why spend time building another food delivery app?

But with that opportunity comes responsibility. Whether the kind of world that gets invented will be beneficial for most people depends on the choices business leaders, investors, and governments make. These will be big, difficult choices about the accountability of technology, the role of education, the nature of government, and even the definition of a person. We'll need to make sure the revolution benefits society broadly, not just the wealthy or the technologically advanced.

At the same time, these new technologies will be able to have an unprecedented impact on each individual's life, and that requires thinking about responsible innovation on a very different, very personal level. I'll address that in the next chapter.

CHAPTER 4

INNOVATE FOR INDIVIDUAL IMPACT

Today's unscaled technologies impact individuals in ways that are far more profound and intimate than ever before. And with that comes a weighty responsibility.

Some of the most important companies of the next couple of decades will be those that use technology to solve persistent personal problems—addiction, financial struggles, health issues, work success, fitness, and overall well-being, to name a few. Yet with that kind of highly personal impact, companies must be sentries against unintended consequences.

Consider the case of Robinhood Financial from the previous chapter. While the company was already getting adverse attention from regulators in 2020, the biggest reputational hit came when a 20-year-old committed suicide after ringing up a negative $730,000 balance in his account. That tragedy turns up in nearly every news story about Robinhood. The man's parents are suing. It is a permanent black mark on the company—and rightfully so.

As described earlier, unscaled technology creates intimacy and empathy at scale. We now spend much of our lives online—shopping, learning, communicating, getting directions, finding romance, and on and on. Every click or swipe we make on an app generates data about us. We carry mobile devices that know where we are. We wear gadgets that can track our health. All of that data can move through the cloud to AI software that can get to know us. That can seem Big Brother-ish, but it's also amazing: It means companies can give us products and services tailored to each of us.

It's the opposite of last century's industries, which strived to make the most of the same thing for the most people—mass production, mass markets, mass media. Scaled industries changed our lives, of course, but they tended to change *everyone's* lives in much the same way. This century's unscaled technologies impact each user's life in a highly personal way.

That means there are opportunities as never before to solve difficult human problems, and entrepreneurs and innovators are now called to do just that. But it is their duty to anticipate unintended consequences and do everything they can to make sure their products do good. Radical empathy is crucial. In this new era, every single user is your company's partner. Lift your partners up and they will in turn lift you up. You can bring them down, but if you do, even just one can hurt you. As Robinhood learned.

———

One of the widespread problems for unscaled companies to solve right now is, ironically, helping people left behind by the shift from the scaled economy to the unscaled economy.

During the past 15 years, millions of people have found they lack the skills to succeed in this new era. Wealth gaps have widened. Unemployment is soaring while hundreds of thousands of jobs go unfilled because too many people have the wrong skills and not enough have the right skills. People getting left behind this way is a giant societal problem—and it's a very personal problem for every individual experiencing it.

Rachel Carlson saw this problem and realized technology could help solve it. She grew up civic-minded, the granddaughter of Roy Romer, a three-term governor of Colorado, and daughter of Chris Romer, a Colorado state senator. Both men had helped start businesses in the adult education space, so as Carlson was finishing her MBA at Stanford, she began thinking about, as she says, "How to help low-income Americans who are going to have to upskill or else they'll be left unemployable. There had to be creative ways to help without having those students bear the costs."[1]

Carlson put some ideas together and in 2015 founded Guild Education. One big insight was that hundreds of terrific nonprofit community colleges have trouble luring enough students. Big for-profit universities, like University of Phoenix, have greatly bid up prices of advertising on platforms such as Google and Facebook, leading the cost of acquiring a single undergraduate student to spike to around $5,000. Carlson believed that if Guild Education could build a better way for those nonprofit colleges to find students, they would gladly pay a fraction of their online advertising budget instead of handing that money to the world's Googles and Facebooks.

Carlson also knew that many companies offer education benefits to employees, yet few use those benefits. She realized employers could get low-income students into community college programs looking for students. If employers reimburse some or all of the tuition, and colleges pay to acquire a student, then Guild could build a business helping low-income students take courses and get degrees for free. Everyone could benefit: employers get better-skilled employees; employees gain new skills and become more marketable; and nonprofit community colleges get more students at a lower cost . . . helping make the colleges healthier so they can offer more and better programs to help yet more adults get ahead.

Walmart, Disney, and Chipotle are some of Guild's biggest clients. But the most dramatic impact is on individuals. Guild's software gets inputs from and data about an employee and uses it to understand that person's goals and challenges. Humans are also there to help when the software can't. The software absorbs details of the company's education benefits program and has a database of schools and courses that the benefits would cover. If a Walmart truck driver with a high school education worries that autonomous vehicles will put him out of work, Guild will help him use Walmart's benefits to get a college degree that puts him on a more promising career path. If he struggles with his courses, Guild's software steps in as a coach.

Guild set up its business model so its intentions—to help individuals have more successful careers—match its incentives. The company gets paid by colleges only when a student completes their classes or program. "If the student drops out or loses their job or isn't successful, don't pay us anymore," Carlson says. "We have this value called 'scale for students, students for scale.' If we're scaling the business, we're doing it for our students, and if we're serving our students well, we're scaling. It's the same sort of concept of 'do well by doing good.'"

That kind of responsible innovation helps Guild avoid unintended consequences—and it also makes for a good business. In 2019, Guild raised a $157 million investment round, valuing the company at more than $1 billion. In May 2020, in the midst of the pandemic, it bought education tech firm Entangled Group for $80 million in stock. Guild used the acquisition to build a matching system for laid-off workers to both get retraining and find new jobs—continuing Guild's mission to innovate for individual impact.

———

For all the good the scaled-up economy of the past century did for quality of life, it took away a human touch. In the scaled economy, the way to serve the growing masses was to standardize products and services—give the same thing to everybody, rely on processes, put everyone on the same schedule, and make humans conform to the system rather than the other way around. So, retail evolved from the local shopkeeper who knew you and knew what you liked, to massive, impersonal Walmart superstores. Healthcare went from a family doctor who saw you throughout your life to giant hospital systems that can feel more like medical factories. The teller who knew you at the local savings and loan has become a global bank's ATM. The small-town, one-room schoolhouse morphed into massive entities like the Los Angeles Unified School District, which has nearly 500,000 students spread across 785 schools.

Today, technology can reverse that trend. Healthcare technology can get to know your health through data and make your care feel more compassionate and personal, like from the family doctor. Similar dynamics are happening in nearly every industry, allowing entrepreneurs to reinvent the way we live and work. Instead of standardized products and services, we get products and services made for each of us. Instead of having to go to school at 8 a.m. on Monday or be in the office from 9 a.m. to 5 p.m. or shop when a store is open, we can do anything at any time. Technology is conforming to humans, not the reverse.

That shift is opening up fascinating opportunities to innovate for individual impact and to build business models that do better when our lives get better, avoiding harmful consequences.

Healthcare may be the biggest opportunity—and the most daunting when it comes to unintended consequences. If a healthcare application fails to work correctly, someone could die. If biases creep into the AI behind health applications, it could mislead certain people based on their gender, race, or age, potentially damaging their health.

Nonetheless, traditional healthcare has been such a terrible experience that there is now an enormous need for innovation that puts the consumer experience first. It's a concept called health assurance. Livongo, which I mentioned earlier, is an example of that model. Traditional healthcare treats all people with diabetes pretty much the same, with care that is episodic, impersonal, and factory-like. Patients are largely left to manage their conditions on their own, so they have to constantly think about it . . . or risk winding up in an emergency room. Livongo instead uses technology to get to know that person's diabetes and then provide guidance that can help the user control the condition and stay out of doctor's offices and hospitals. As Livongo builds trust, the user feels a peace of mind and can push diabetes management—and engagement with Livongo—to the background. Livongo makes money when its users stay healthier and spend less on healthcare, helping align the business model incentives with intentions. Its users tend to spend less on healthcare and feel happier than before they got involved with the service.

In 2020, Teledoc agreed to merge with Livongo in an $18.5 billion deal—the biggest exit to date for a next-generation health tech company. It's proof that responsibly innovating for individual impact in healthcare is a good business model.

The past few years have seen a surge in startups that innovate for individual impact across many aspects of healthcare. Nuvo, out of Israel, is using the cloud, connected devices, and AI to give women more control and information with a new category of technology it calls "connected pregnancy care." Cityblock has created a business model that makes it profitable to help low-income and homeless people get better care and stay healthier. Seattle-based Trainiac has built a model it calls "individualized fitness"—a cloud-based service that uses technology and human trainers to guide users through workouts designed specifically for them.

Finance is another industry ripe for innovating for individual impact. Banks have left a great deal of the population behind, all over the world. Major banks have a business model that makes personal banking more personalized and cheaper for people with a lot of money, but costly and industrialized for people with low incomes. Many poor people don't use banks at all. That leaves room for startups that offer the kind of personalized financial guidance that's typically only offered to wealthy customers. Lenddo, based in Singapore, built an AI that analyzes a person's social media presence to determine whether that person is creditworthy. That helps people in developing countries who never had a bank account or credit card to get a loan to, say, start a business or send a child to school. Lemonade is reinventing insurance by making it personal and affordable. The pitch on its site: "Maya, our charming artificial intelligence bot, will craft the perfect insurance for you." Such companies are building good businesses by remaking finance to help close wealth gaps and make the economy more equitable.

I'm sure we'll see companies innovating in every facet of our lives—reinventing the way we approach food, fashion, relationships, travel, workplace skills, education, and on and on. The next wave of billion-dollar companies will be those that develop business models that create positive impact on a deeply personal level, making sure their incentives align with ensuring the technology does good and does not veer into damaging consequences.

———

We've all seen what not to do when it comes to innovating for individual impact because it's what some of the world's most successful companies do every day. Instagram, owned by Facebook, is a prime example. Its business model relies on advertising and influence—in other words, in manipulating our behavior. To make the most money, it must drive engagement—or, more accurately, addiction. The business model gives the company incentives to have a harmful individual impact. And that harmful impact has become obvious.

Instagram has become a place to show off idealized versions of our lives. Teenage girls are particularly vulnerable to this. Of Instagram's one billion users worldwide, about 60 percent are females under age 34. The site plays on young women's fear of missing out, of not conforming, of not looking good enough. One study showed that among young women and girls, "the frequency of Instagram use is correlated with depressive symptoms, self-esteem, general and physical appearance anxiety, and body dissatisfaction."[2] By any measure, Instagram fails the responsible innovation test. It is engineered for negative individual impact. The company started out as a photo-sharing site, but its unintended consequences quickly turned ugly.

While Instagram is an in-your-face example of harming individual lives, companies also have to be attuned to more subtle unintended consequences, particularly when it comes to biases that get infused into AI.

One example is from a study of how Boston-area hospitals were using an algorithm to determine who should get kidney transplants.[3] The technology was intended to have a positive individual impact by identifying the most critical patients with kidney disease and making sure that scarce kidney transplants went to those who needed it most. But the study found that a bias in the algorithm scored Black people differently from White people. "One-third of Black patients, more than 700 people, would have been placed into a more severe category of kidney disease if their kidney function had been estimated using the same formula as for white patients," the study found. Instead, those Black people were put in line behind less-critical White patients. The bias that crept into the algorithm cost people their lives.

How, then, can companies think about innovating for positive, profound individual impact while steering clear of unintended consequences?

Start with radical empathy. That means deeply thinking through what your end users want and need to make their lives better. The goal of engagement—for so long the tech industry's holy grail—runs counter to what your users need. Engagement means manipulating people so they use your product or service more. As soon as you do that, you've gotten off the track of focusing on solving your users' problems and improving their lives. The better you solve their problems, the less likely they are to engage with your product or service.

Second, develop a business model that ensures the company makes more money by having a positive individual impact. That probably eliminates advertising as the chief source of revenue, because your real customer is the advertisers and the incentive is to please them, not your end users. Guild Education solved this by developing an innovative business model that makes more money when it does a better job helping more people get educated. Livongo gets paid when its users manage their conditions better and need less traditional healthcare. Netflix makes all its money on subscriptions, which incentivizes the company to give viewers satisfying entertainment instead of lowest-common-denominator sitcoms and reality shows.

And, finally, plan to endure and infuse that mindset into everything the company does. Because innovating for individual impact by definition means your product or service can deeply affect individual lives. The stakes are high when it comes to unintended consequences, as Robinhood learned when that young man committed suicide. It's not likely any company can have great individual impact *and* endure (and not get hauled before Congress to testify) unless it avoids harmful unintended consequences. So planning to endure for generations to come necessarily dictates that companies must pay attention to and avoid unintended consequences.

CHAPTER 5

FIGHT INEQUALITY

If the technologies today's companies are developing can help solve big, complex societal issues that have been unsolvable for decades, then it is incumbent upon entrepreneurs to start companies that solve such problems. But they don't need to do that simply out of duty. Solving big, complex societal problems can be a path to building great, enduring, responsible companies.

One hard-to-solve societal issue is inequality. History and market capitalism have played off one another to create enormous and growing wealth and opportunity gaps.[1] We all know that the top 1 percent have left the other 99 percent far behind, but data collected by the Federal Reserve Bank of St. Louis shows the shocking reality of the gap. The top 1 percent in 2020 held 31 percent of all net worth in the United States.[2] The top 10 percent owned 76 percent of household wealth. Black families' median and mean wealth is less than 15 percent that of White families.[3] About 39 percent of US families have at least one member with a college degree, and those families hold about 77 percent of total wealth. Basically, if you're anything but White and college-educated, you start out at a disadvantage. Anyone not already in the 1 percent is going to have a difficult time getting there.

And the pandemic exacerbated wealth gaps. From early 2020 to mid-2021, stock prices and home values soared, helping the top 1 percent, who own the majority of stocks and high-priced homes. At the same time, many of the bottom 50 percent—often people with jobs in service industries—lost income. Since the start of 2020, the bottom 50 percent gained about $700 billion in wealth. The richest 1 percent gained $10 trillion.[4]

Government has shown it is unable or unwilling to close such gaps. Companies, many following Friedman's doctrine of shareholder primacy, have mostly made the gaps worse. A new generation of companies can do better.

There are two ways for companies to whittle away at wealth and opportunity gaps by solving for inequality and inclusion.

One is to build a business explicitly designed to improve life and opportunity for those who are disadvantaged. There are many clever ways to use technology to give a better chance to those who need it, and do it profitably.

The other path is to consider what happens inside a company. It might be in any business, perhaps doing nothing that particularly helps disadvantaged people. But it can still help solve for inequality and inclusion through the way it pays employees, how it hires and promotes, how it runs business day to day, and the overall culture it nurtures.

Here are stories of both kinds of companies.

————

Toyin Ajayi is a family doctor by training. She worked in community health centers that often served what she terms "marginalized patients"—people at the edges of society, such as the homeless or those with addictions or mental health issues. Then, for four years she worked for a health insurance company trying to figure out how to better serve that same population. She learned how money flows in healthcare, saw how the traditional healthcare industry is failing marginalized populations, and believed there had to be a better way to help people. Failing to solve this problem costs society hundreds of billions of dollars because marginalized people often wind up in emergency rooms getting the highest-cost treatments, yet are unable to pay their medical bills.

In 2016, healthcare veteran Iyah Romm got a call from Dan Doctoroff, who runs Google's Sidewalk Labs. He asked him to come work on ideas for a company that might tackle this problem. Romm brought in Ajayi, and out of that work, they formed Cityblock Health inside of Sidewalk Labs, and then spun it out as an independent startup in 2017. In late 2020, Cityblock raised $160 million and is worth north of $1 billion.[5]

Cityblock is clearly a responsible innovation company: It set out to solve the inherent inequality and exclusion in healthcare as well as lower the cost of healthcare to society. To accomplish that, the company had to build a profitable, scalable business so it could endure and have a significant impact. An admirable purpose alone wouldn't be enough—Cityblock needed a mechanism that would support that purpose for decades to come. "There was a dearth of innovation in this space," Ajayi says. "I believed in the model we came up with."[6]

Cityblock's key insight is that it can use technology to find marginalized patients and help them consistently take better care of themselves so they don't get sick as often and wind up in emergency rooms. To make money, Cityblock offers a deal to the insurers who end up paying marginalized patients' bills. The insurer gives Cityblock a lump sum of what a patient's healthcare would normally cost—which could be as much as $20,000 a year. Cityblock then takes responsibility for all of that patient's healthcare spending. If Cityblock can keep the patient healthier and the patient only uses $10,000 worth of healthcare, Cityblock keeps the money it saves, sharing some of that with the insurer (which gives the insurer motivation to sign up with Cityblock).

Mobile devices and cloud services help track patients and provide virtual care. To see the service from the perspective of a patient, Ajayi says, consider someone who may be homeless or doesn't have a fixed address, may often be in unsafe situations, has no insurance and little income, rarely sees a primary care doctor, and has any number of underlying conditions, such as hypertension or diabetes. In the typical healthcare system, if that person has chest pains or similar health issues, he or she goes to the ER and gets costly tests. "They're touching the hospital all the time but getting sicker," she says.

Once a patient is assigned to Cityblock, the person gets a call or someone goes to meet him or her. "They meet someone who often looks like them, from the neighborhood," Ajayi says. "It's not a medical conversation—it's just to find out what's going on with you. Build toward trust. And we develop an action plan. 'Next time you're hungry, come by our hub for something to eat. You don't have an ID, we'll get you one.' That may lead to, 'Come in and get a mammogram; we'll make it easy.' " If they have a cell phone, they can talk to a nurse, doctor, or mental health professional anytime. Making patients' lives more stable and giving them someone to talk to about health issues dramatically decreases their healthcare spend. Even just helping patients get medications and consistently take them vastly reduces their need for expensive care.

Cityblock is making a profit by helping everyone in its chain: the patient, the hospital, the insurer, and the community. It's a classic example of setting up a mechanism to support a mindset.

Another startup, Ossium Health, is aiming to lessen inequality in healthcare in a very different way. Stem cells have become a promising way to treat a vast range of diseases, including some cancers, HIV, and autoimmune diseases like multiple sclerosis. Each year, about 30,000 patients in the United States get an organ transplant and then have to take expensive drugs the rest of their lives to prevent their bodies from rejecting the organ. A single round of stem cell therapy could end the need for those drugs.

The problem is that stem cells are hard to get and cultivate. Today, if a patient needs stem cell treatments, the cells are harvested from his or her bloodstream—a difficult process that involves taking drugs for four or five days to move the cells from the bone marrow into the bloodstream. Then the blood is collected in sessions that take three or more hours each day for three or four days, and the stem cells are separated out. This is not a process that can be done in an emergency or on someone who is already very sick. Another option would be to get matching stem cells from another person, but finding such a match now is supremely difficult—no one has created a big enough supply of stem cells nor the data about them to quickly establish a match. All of that makes stem cell therapy costly—and available mainly to wealthier patients.[7]

"So we thought, what if it becomes easier and cheaper to get access to those cells?" says Kevin Caldwell, Ossium's CEO. "What if you could order those on demand? Get as many as you want—prescreened, all the data available?" If all that were possible, the cost of treating diseases would plummet, making a huge impact on health across the broad population. As Ossium's website says, the company is in business "with the ultimate goal of ending disease."[8]

That's a worthy mindset. But what mechanism can make that work—and avoid the unintended consequence of making a product for the rich, further opening up the yawning health gap between rich and poor?

For that, Ossium needs a lot of stem cells, which means it needs a new way to get them. About half of Americans are registered as organ donors—when they die, their organs may be removed and used in transplants. In most cases, the bone marrow is discarded, not considered valuable. But bone marrow contains stem cells. So Ossium started by working with the organ transplant ecosystem to add one more step: harvesting the marrow for stem cells.

Ossium also needs data about those cells. Not all stem cells are the same, nor will any stem cell work in any person. Ossium has to create a database of cells and use the data to learn about the best ways to put those cells to work.

Put it all together and Ossium is developing an on-demand bank of stem cells that can be ready for use in a variety of treatments and is easily accessible to physicians, hospitals, researchers, and biotech companies.

"Inevitably, when you do something new, it can be extraordinarily expensive," Caldwell notes. "Those costs will come down over time, but time alone isn't enough for us. We can accelerate the pace of getting the cost down and making it available to more people."

Caldwell believes Ossium can be a far more profitable business if it can help find ways to use stem cells to treat a broad range of diseases at low cost for almost everybody—a massive volume business instead of a pricey niche business. The data flywheel is an important part of that: the more the cells are used in treatments, the more data comes back that helps Ossium learn more about the cells . . . so it can help develop more and better treatments. "The positive incentive is for us to make this as widely available as possible," Caldwell says.

The mechanism Ossium has set up supports the company's mindset and steers it away from decisions that might widen health gaps. As Ossium makes stem cell therapies cheaper, better, and more accessible, it can learn how to make stem cell therapies even cheaper, better, and more accessible—a cycle that promises to flatten out inequality in healthcare while generating profits.

Until recently, many companies considered diversity a "nice to have." Companies supported diversity and inclusion because they wanted to be good citizens, because it was the right thing to do, and—for some, cynically—because it was good PR. But now research is proving the business case for diversity and inclusion. It's not just nice to have—it's critical to building a great, enduring company. Creating a diverse and inclusive culture is essentially its own business mechanism for solving for diversity and inclusion.

Leading consulting firms are emphatic about this point. Deloitte reports that "research shows that diversity of thinking is a wellspring of creativity, enhancing innovation by about 20 percent. It enables groups to spot risks, reducing these by up to 30 percent." A 2018 McKinsey study of companies around the world discovered similar results. "[C]ompanies with the most ethnically diverse executive teams are 33 percent more likely to outperform their peers on profitability." And there's a penalty for not being diverse: "Companies in the fourth quartile on both gender and ethnic diversity are more likely to underperform their industry peers on profitability [by] 29 percent."[9]

Amazon and Netflix are two of the most admired companies in tech—admired not just for their astounding success, but for the way they are run. The two companies understand, or at least communicate, the business case for diversity and inclusion. "Our work has to be internal first, so it can impact what we do externally," according to Netflix's website. "We believe we'll do that better if our employees come from different backgrounds, and if we create an environment of inclusion and belonging for them."[10] Netflix's diversity helps it develop content that appeals to all kinds of people, everywhere in the world. It also helps the company understand how to deliver that content to anyone who wants it—"removing the barriers of language, device, ability or connectivity."

How does Netflix achieve diversity? A great deal of it comes from hiring and promoting with diversity and inclusion in mind. The company reports that its employee base is about 45 percent White, 9 percent Black, 8 percent Hispanic, 24 percent Asian, and the rest a mix of other ethnicities. And its employees are about evenly split between men and women. The leadership team is about 57 percent White, evenly split between men and women. Once people are inside Netflix, according to the company, it's important to make them "feel like they have a home here." To help with that, Netflix created Employee Resource Groups such as Black@Netflix and Dream@Netflix (for "immigrant populations and allies").

The company's overall point is that to excel, Netflix must nurture a culture that values diversity not just because it's right, but because it is good for business.

Amazon also believes in the business case for its diversity mindset. The company has its "Amazon pledge," which begins: "Diversity and inclusion are good for business—and more fundamentally—simply right. Customers represent a wide array of genders, races, ethnicities, abilities, ages, religions, sexual orientations, military status, backgrounds, and political views. It's critical that Amazon employees are also diverse and that we foster a culture where inclusion is the norm."[11]

The company reports that in 2020 its US workforce was 32 percent White, 27 percent Black, 23 percent Hispanic, and 14 percent Asian.[12] The management level skewed White (56 percent) and less diverse. Male employees outnumbered females, 55 percent to 45 percent. Also like Netflix, Amazon seems to understand that just having diverse employees isn't enough— they must also feel at home and that they have an equal voice in the business. An employee survey led the company to this definition of inclusion: "Being valued, trusted, connected, and informed so that we can deliver the best results for our customers."[13] And Amazon uses that definition to guide it when developing programs and benefits that foster an inclusive culture. (Whether the programs are succeeding is up for debate: Some press accounts in 2021 said Blacks were systematically kept out of senior positions.[14] Amazon denied the allegations.)

Internal diversity when serving a diverse world makes obvious business sense, but the business case for closing the economic gap between higher-paying jobs and lower-paying jobs is more nuanced.

Dan Schulman joined PayPal as CEO in 2014. In his previous position as a group president at American Express, he funded a documentary called *Spent: Looking for Change*, about the difficulties of being one of America's unbanked.[15] When he came to PayPal, he declared that the company's mission would go beyond giving people a way to send money around. He wanted to "make financial services universally affordable and accessible." If PayPal was going to do that for the world at large, Schulman declared, it had to have that same sensitivity to the struggles of the lowest-paid PayPal employees.

In 2017, Schulman established an "employee relief fund" to aid lower-level workers experiencing financial trouble. He initiated a survey of employees in 2018 and found that 60 percent of workers had little extra money for emergencies or education. The 2020 pandemic added a new level of financial stress to those workers, as many faced mounting healthcare costs while at the same time being asked to work harder for the same pay, since the pandemic set off a PayPal boom as more commerce shifted online.

Schulman realized he had to do something about the large gap between the lower-paid employees and the rest of the company. "Imagine asking people to double down on serving customers when they're more financially stressed than ever before, when they don't even have healthcare benefits," he told *Insider*.[16] So PayPal raised wages for lower-level workers by about 7 percent—not a huge amount, but enough to ease money worries—and gave them restricted stock units so they could share in PayPal's success. The company also covered more healthcare costs, cutting the amount lower-level employees contribute by around 58 percent.

What happened? Employee turnover has been cut in half, which means that experienced employees stay, while saving the company the costs of recruiting and training new workers.

PayPal grew at a record pace in 2020 and the stock price more than doubled that year. Perhaps the company would've done as well if it had never instituted programs to address financial inequality, but Schulman believes the policies paid for themselves, and they left PayPal with a reputation as a great place to work. Glassdoor has PayPal at a 4.1 rating (out of a possible 5) with 4,500 reviews, and Schulman has a 94 percent approval rating as of this writing.

The companies that solve for diversity and inclusion internally tend to make the best products, innovate faster, avoid unintended consequences, lure top talent, and, in the end, have the best business outcomes—all while helping close society's wealth and opportunity gaps. No founder or CEO can ignore those results.

CHAPTER 6

TAKE RESPONSIBILITY FOR CLIMATE CHANGE

Picture Henry Ford calling his leadership team into a working session on responsible innovation and unintended consequences as the Model T was about to roll out in 1908. The challenge would have been to look at their business model and answer this question: What if we succeed beyond our wildest dreams?

Just thinking about this scenario shows how tough it is to predict ramifications. How could anyone in 1908 have predicted six-lane highways, rush-hour traffic jams, 18-wheelers, and Hummers? Still, the Ford team might've realized back then that the whole reason behind the Model T was to build a car that everyone could own. The company's business model was to sell as many cars to as many people as possible. So, if everyone owned a car (or two), what would be the potential negative consequences? Maybe the Ford team would have considered the fumes pouring out of Model T tailpipes and wondered what would happen to the air once millions of cars were on the road. If cars made people more mobile, might employees move farther from work and have to drive more? Even though more cars and more driving would benefit the Ford business model, would there be a cost to society and the environment?

And then, if by some magic Henry Ford and his executives had foreseen pollution, urban sprawl, choked interstates, and climate change resulting from vehicles powered by oil-burning internal combustion engines—would they have altered their business model? Explored electric cars? Ford had no computer models to help the company peer into the future, as might happen today, but imagine if one of us could go back in time and tell Henry Ford he was about to set in motion events that would bring the world to the brink of climate disaster while his great-grandchildren were still alive. What would he have done?

As we all now understand, twentieth-century technology, from cars to coal-fired electric plants, has been largely responsible for the crisis of climate change. Data centers have become some of the largest consumers of energy, which means that the technology sector has become one of the biggest carbon polluters. (An unintended consequence!) Now, this century's technology needs to help solve the problems we've created.

No call to action for technology founders could be more important. It's the ultimate goal in responsible innovation. If we have the opportunity and capability to curtail climate change and don't do it, the whole world will suffer, economies will get crushed, and the ecosystem necessary for businesses to thrive will break apart like an ice floe in a heat wave.

But it's counterproductive to only think of addressing climate change as a duty. It's also a fantastic opportunity, spread throughout every nook and cranny of every industry—an opportunity that's getting more attractive every day. This goes far beyond ESG—environmental, social, and corporate governance—though ESG has created awareness among investors and spurred corporations and governments to action.

In March 2021, President Biden launched a trillion-dollar plan to get the United States to net-zero carbon emissions by 2050. The trillion-dollar plan includes money and incentives to build a grid for renewable energy, electric vehicle charging stations, battery technology, and energy-efficient housing. At the plan's rollout, Biden argued that climate-focused businesses are the future font of good jobs. Representative Alexandria Ocasio-Cortez, Democrat of New York, told the *New York Times*: "One of the big goals we had when we introduced the Green New Deal was to shift climate change from being a billion-dollar problem to a trillion-dollar opportunity."[1] Meanwhile, more than 60 countries and 100 cities around the world have adopted net-zero carbon emission targets.

Investors are on board. Nearly 400 investors representing more than $35 trillion in assets under management signed the Climate Action 100+ initiative, which demands that corporate greenhouse gas emitters "curb emissions, improve governance and strengthen climate-related financial disclosures."[2]

As governments and corporations look to improve environmental performance, they'll need innovations from startups. That's why venture capital (VC) investment in climate-related companies is exploding, growing from $418 million in 2013 to $16.3 billion in 2019—and beyond that in 2020, according to a PWC report.[3] That's three times the growth rate of VC investment into AI technologies, the report says.[4]

There are the obvious climate-oriented businesses to build—electric cars, solar energy, biofuels, carbon removal, and so on. Less obvious opportunities are almost limitless.

For instance, making manufacturing and farming more efficient will drive down energy use. Zoom is making business travel less necessary. Impossible Foods is making methane-spewing cows less necessary. Oxford Photovoltaics, which claims it invented breakthrough solar energy cells that are much more efficient than any now available, raised $120 million. Energy General Fusion, which says it is "developing the first commercially-viable fusion power plant," raised $136 million in 2020. Planet Labs, maker of small satellites that can look at things like crops and urban planning to generate insights about climate change, raised a round that valued the company at $2.2 billion and, in summer 2021, was making plans to go public. The category of "micromobility"—electric scooters and bikes and self-driving delivery robots—is a burgeoning sector, with companies raising more than $9 billion from 2013 to 2019.[5]

I'm certain dozens of $100 billion companies addressing climate change in some way will get built, and a few will become the next generation's Apple, Google, or Microsoft.

Tesla, as I described earlier, is showing the way to monster success. Keep in mind that Elon Musk didn't set out to just build a cool car company. He thinks about his company as an integrated energy and transportation entity. Musk in 2016 published his "Master Plan, Part Deux" (a sequel to his first Master Plan, published in 2006).[6] He wrote that Tesla built hot electric cars as an entry point for ending dependence on oil. "The point of all this was, and remains, accelerating the advent of sustainable energy, so that we can imagine far into the future and life is still good." Tesla cars will be a part of a sustainable electric system that includes solar panels, batteries, and software to manage power and trade it over networks.

The other side of developing technologies that address climate change is making sure we don't build technologies that create unintended consequences that make the situation worse. Case in point: bitcoin. Just a few years ago, bitcoin was heralded as a breakthrough technology that was going to reinvent money for a new age. Now bitcoin gets disparaged as a climate disaster. Bitcoin miners across the globe use tremendous amounts of electricity on computing power. "Bitcoin uses more electricity per transaction than any other method known to mankind, and so it's not a great climate thing," Bill Gates said in a live Clubhouse session.[7] A Bank of America report says that bitcoin's energy consumption is comparable to that of a major corporation like American Airlines, which flies more than 200 million passengers a year.

Nearly as insidious is greenwashing—making climate promises that don't get met. A mindset of pledging to be carbon neutral is a precarious promise if it's not supported by mechanisms that make climate-friendly policies profitable. Otherwise, companies will abandon their good intentions under financial pressure.

As I've said throughout this book, mindset has to be supported by mechanisms. Henry Ford built a business model mechanism that ensured his company would lead to climate change. Today's companies must build mechanisms that reverse the damage.

"Environmental stewardship is consistent with a capitalist approach," says Nat Kreamer, CEO of the nonprofit group Advanced Energy Economy (which I cofounded with Tom Steyer a decade ago). Consider, Kreamer says, a factory dealing with lots of intermittent, unplanned downtime that stalls production. If demand for the company's products increases, it would have to build another plant, and that would add to the company's carbon footprint—everything from plant construction to more electricity use. If the company could get rid of the downtime and optimize factory usage, it could meet demand, make more profit, and throw off less carbon. " 'Faster, cheaper, better' uses less resources," Kreamer says. "And 'faster, cheaper, better' drives profit."

As manufacturers seek those efficiencies, there are opportunities for companies to help with the "faster, cheaper, better." This is the chance a startup called Guidewheel (previously known as Safi) jumped on, and the company illustrates how a business-driven mechanism can be leveraged to reduce carbon emissions.

Guidewheel's story: In the early 2010s, Lauren Dunford graduated from Stanford and joined Revolution Foods, which makes and ships healthy lunches to schools across the country. Revolution Foods was a comparatively small manufacturer, and it tracked its processes the way a lot of smaller manufacturers do: with paper, spreadsheets, and sticky notes. After she left the company, Dunford returned to Stanford to get an MBA. Compelled to do something about climate change, she focused on studying issues around supply chain efficiency and carbon footprint. Dunford also happened to be married to Jason Dunford, who was born in Kenya and swam for the Kenyan Olympic team. After business school, the couple moved to Kenya, where she saw an economy dominated by small manufacturers, most operating by paper and clipboard. All of this led her to realize that thousands of small and medium-size manufacturers around the world were operating inefficiently and wasting great amounts of energy.

Wanting to do something about that, Dunford cofounded Guidewheel. The solution it would offer had to be cheap and easy for a small manufacturer to install and use—most don't have the budget or personnel to take on a big, complex technology project. So Guidewheel developed a wireless sensor that can clip on any electric wire, read the electric current going through it, and send that data through the cloud to software that can look for patterns. Turns out that patterns of electricity use can show which machines in the factory will go down or are running inefficiently, which helps managers find ways to save energy.

Except, as Dunford found out, just saving energy doesn't sell well. "We built this intuitive energy management system, but most customers don't care about energy on a daily basis," she says. However, Guidewheel realized the same patterns that reveal idle times and manufacturing hiccups give managers a way to reduce downtime and optimize the factory so the plant can make more products and earn more profit. "We redesigned the system for that, and now use it as a Trojan horse for energy efficiency," Dunford says. "Customers won't use it unless it solves something they care about"—like profit. Guidewheel now markets its system as "a plug-and-play platform that gives any factory team the tools to get to operational excellence quickly, cost-effectively, and simply."[8]

Dunford started with the idea of reducing the carbon footprint of factories. She found a mechanism to make it work: selling a system that helps smaller manufacturers make more money by operating more efficiently and thereby saving energy. Sometimes the right mechanism isn't immediately obvious. But get it right, and it supports the mindset of good intentions.

Indoor data-driven farming is another twist on a business model that helps with climate change in a less obvious way. By 2050, the planet is projected to have 2.2 billion more people to feed, just as global warming is expected to make weather less predictable and dry up previously fertile regions.[9] If food can be grown cost-effectively indoors, in or near cities, climate will be less of a concern, and far less carbon will be burned while moving food thousands of miles via trucks, trains, and ships. Indoor farming startups are sprouting globally. Plenty, based in San Francisco, raised $401 million in funding with backers such as SoftBank, Alphabet chairman Eric Schmidt, and Amazon CEO Jeff Bezos. US startups AeroFarms and Bowery Farming have raised $238 million and $167.5 million, respectively.[10] According to New York–based BrightFarms, it "finances, designs, builds, and operates" indoor farms close to food retailers and has raised $11 million in funding. Formerly Edenworks, Upward Farms' rooftop greenhouses grow produce fertilized by ground tilapia and prawns, which are also grown at the minifarm.

Bowery and AeroFarms are both in old industrial buildings in New Jersey, a short drive from New York City.[11] Inside these buildings, LED lights mimic sunlight. The crops grow in nutrient-rich water beds on trays stacked floor to ceiling.

Sensors constantly monitor the plants and send data back to AI-driven software, which can learn what's best for the plants and tweak lighting, water, and fertilizer to improve yield. "We get productivity hundreds of times greater than a traditional farm," says AeroFarms CEO David Rosenberg. "And we use less water and no pesticides—because we're indoors—and can grow 365 days a year." This new generation of farming promises to feed more people while doing less environmental damage. This isn't traditional farms operating on good intentions—it's reimagining farms with business models geared toward making profits while also helping the planet.

Changes in societal attitudes and environmental regulations have also created opportunities to tackle climate change head-on. Founders are starting companies that would have sounded crazy just a decade ago.

One of those is Charm Industrial, founded by Peter Reinhardt, who in 2020 sold his previous company, Segment, to Twilio for $3.2 billion.[12] Charm Industrial is building technology for "bio-oil sequestration"—not a phrase people bandy about in bars. Basically, it means taking agricultural waste—biomass that would ordinarily release carbon into the atmosphere—and converting it to what Reinhardt calls "shitty oil" that's no good for fuel or anything else. The shitty oil is then injected deep underground—preventing it from adding to climate change. And it can do that more cheaply than most any other method of carbon removal. (According to Charm Industrial, it can do that at 40 percent less than other technologies, and it will get even cheaper.)

So how is that a business? Charm's main market today is companies that want to do "voluntary" carbon removal— potentially a $500 million market annually. But "voluntary" is becoming a misnomer. Yes, these companies aren't doing it to meet a regulatory requirement. But it's becoming a necessity. A new generation wants to work for climate-friendly companies. Making a net-zero carbon emissions pledge has become vital to hiring all the best people. ESG investors want to put their money in climate-friendly companies. Consumers increasingly care and say they will buy from climate-friendly companies. Increasingly, the most successful companies will be those that take carbon reduction seriously.[13]

Online payments company Stripe was one of Charm's first customers. Stripe doesn't have a way to capture its carbon emissions and bury them. Instead, it buys an amount of carbon from other sources equivalent to its emissions, and then has Charm turn it into shitty, permanently buried oil.

Stripe's model for addressing climate change could be a model for how other companies not in the business of climate change can help develop technology for climate change.

In 2019, the company created Stripe Climate, a kind of investment skunkworks inside of Stripe, run by Nan Ransohoff. The thinking behind Stripe Climate: The only way to turn back climate change will be carbon removal from the atmosphere, not just ending carbon emissions. But almost all carbon removal technology is early stage and expensive, so there is little demand for these solutions—which means these start-ups have trouble getting customers or investors. And without demand, the technologies can't get perfected and scaled up so the costs come down. It's a classic chicken-egg problem.

So, Stripe teed up a $1 million fund to buy overly expensive carbon removal solutions. "We decided we'll pay what we have to pay to help get them down the cost curve," Ransohoff says. "We're making purchases, not investments."

Now, $1 million, in this context, is a pittance. But, Ransohoff says, "It turned out to be a weirdly impactful amount of money."[14] Many of the companies using Stripe wanted to also help with climate change. Stripe set up its platform so an e-commerce company could easily give a small percentage of sales toward carbon removal, with a badge the companies can add to their app or website so they get credit for their donation. As that money pours in, Stripe can buy more from carbon removal companies. If Stripe raises as much money as Ransohoff thinks it will, the company can get into more than just purchasing carbon removal—it could fund research, helping to get ideas out of labs and into the market.

In this model, everyone wins: Stripe makes good on its carbon pledge; the world winds up with less carbon in the atmosphere; a company like Charm Industrial makes a profit so it can continue to develop the technology and serve more customers better and more cheaply. The boost from Stripe means that in time, Reinhardt says, Charm will have the technology to address big industrial sectors like steel, turning biomass into clean-burning fuel for direct use in factories, or capturing and burying biomass for carbon offsets dictated by regulations.

Again, the right kind of capitalism is key. When the business-model mechanism supports the right intentions, good things happen.

PART III

Mechanism: Playbook for Building Responsible Innovation Companies

CHAPTER 7

RESPONSIBLE BUSINESS MODELS

During the past few years, if you took a walk around San Francisco, Seattle, Santa Monica, or Singapore, you likely had to step over electric scooters from Bird or Lime or Scoot that were abandoned, lying on their sides, in the middle of the sidewalk.[1] Or you'd have seen them tossed in the bushes or people's yards or even water fountains. Then, while you were marveling at the site of such a mass beaching of dead scooters, you might have had to jump out of the way of a couple of them being driven down the sidewalk at high speed. At one point, San Diego was cluttered with more than 19,000 scooters and had documented more than 15,000 complaints about them. Because of all this, the scooter companies have found themselves banned in some cities or hated by the residents of others.

The irony is that the scooters were meant to solve big problems, not cause more headaches. They are fast and cheap enough (costing about $3 for a two-mile ride) to get people out of cars for short trips around a city, helping to alleviate carbon emissions, traffic congestion, and parking shortages. Plus, the e-scooters can be fun—certainly more fun than waiting for a bus.

But this is how unintended consequences can creep in when a business model doesn't steer a company around them. Most of the e-scooter business models encouraged the companies to pump as many scooters as possible into a city and place them all around so that a user could always find one nearby. A user would fire up the company's mobile app, and GPS would show where to find nearby scooters. Tap on a scooter and it would unlock and be ready for use. The user would pay per minute of riding. That meant a company would make more money the more minutes its scooters were in use. So, while the mindset was to help cities ease climate change and congestion, the motivation was to blanket the city with as many scooters as possible. That motivation intensified as competition in the space heated up; every company wanted to win the category, creating a race to have the most scooters in town.

It doesn't seem that any e-scooter leadership team considered the question: What if we succeed beyond our dreams? Might they have foreseen a backlash as cool, fun e-scooters became more like a plague of giant locusts? What if the companies had thought through unintended consequences that would become a challenge? And even if they did predict the unintended consequences, most of the companies were set up so that it would have been hard to avoid those consequences. Even the best intentions can be led astray by the wrong incentives.

It's also clear that trying to make up for a problematic business model by launching after-the-fact responsible innovation initiatives doesn't work. Facebook is a prime example. Mark Zuckerberg didn't start Facebook thinking it might someday play a lead role in dividing society and threatening democracy. If the company had stayed private, Zuckerberg would have had the leverage to alter Facebook's business model once he got a glimpse of warning signs. (Whether he would have is another story.) But after the company went public, and the business model that relies on engagement and advertising was set in motion, investors would have punished him—no doubt sued him—if he had made a change that hurt financial results.

So now Facebook is stuck with a business model that rewards the company and investors for its damaging unintended consequences, and Zuckerberg won't/can't change it. In 2020 Facebook set up a team with a mission to assess new Facebook products or features and help prevent them from being misused and causing harm. And yet, Facebook's future relies on launching products and services that will be even more intrusive and manipulative, such as facial recognition that could let someone wear augmented reality glasses that identify who's passing by on the sidewalk. How many ways do you think that could be abused? Facebook's model relies on getting more data about its users, knowing them more precisely, and targeting them personally so they stay in the Facebook universe. To grow, Facebook needs more and more of that. To be responsible, it would have to end such programs and risk slowing growth and a diving stock price.

The public should be wary of companies that say they're trying to be responsible, yet have an underlying model that can derail their best intentions. One example is the dating app Hinge, which founder Justin McLeod famously marketed as "designed to be deleted." One of its slogans was "find love, dump us." In other words, it was pitching disengagement, which is responsible—the app should do the job users expect it to do (find a partner) and then go away. McLeod told *Fast Company*, "We're making a bet that by being the most effective app, we will win the market in the long term."[2] After betting big on its disengagement message, Hinge's revenue nearly tripled in 2020.[3]

And yet . . . Hinge makes money by charging a monthly subscription fee. It makes more money the longer it takes a user to find a partner, and makes yet more money if a partner doesn't work out and the user comes back to Hinge. As long as Hinge is growing by acquiring new customers who like the "designed to be deleted" approach, the mismatch of intentions and incentives might never clash. But if for any reason the company finds itself pressed to find ways to grow, its business model points to engagement—getting users to stay on the app longer, which is directly counter to the user's best interests.

Of course, too many e-scooters on the sidewalk and spending too much time on a dating app are relatively harmless outcomes compared to some of the potential unintended consequences from technologies now being built. Deepfake videos using AI could deceive millions and cause riots or revolutions. Gene-editing technology could wind up creating an invasive species that wrecks the planet's ecosystem. Autonomous weapon-carrying drones guided by bias-infused AI could mistakenly start targeting people with certain ethnic features. Many technologies being developed today can and will vastly improve life for much of the world, but many of those same technologies also have the potential for enormous harm.

Responsible innovation has never been more critical, and the only way to make sure that good intentions win is to back them up with incentives that reward them.

So far in this book, I've detailed several business models that support a responsible innovation mindset with a matching mechanism. Cityblock Health set up a mechanism that lets it profit from improving the health of people left out of the traditional healthcare system, helping society while building a billion-dollar business. Guild Education makes more money when its clientele completes courses, incentivizing the company to follow through on its mission to help people get ahead by getting better educated. Guidewheel makes more money when manufacturers using its products save energy and cut down on waste. Such business models help keep a company on course when temptations to chase revenue imperil good intentions.

Capitalism can be blamed for many of society's ills, like gross economic inequality and the emissions causing climate change. But capitalism can also be a powerful solution for those problems. The trick is in harnessing capitalism for good—for making solutions a profitable opportunity as well as minimizing capitalism's tendency to exploit whatever it can for profit. But that doesn't mean profits and rising stock prices are bad. Set up right, those outcomes can provide incentives to do good things. The key is a business model that matches mindset to mechanism.

So, if you're a company leader, how do you get there? When I look at companies that have matched mindset and mechanism, I see some common practices, the most significant of which are discussed next.

THINK IN INFINITE TIME HORIZONS

This is what Brian Chesky did at Airbnb. He wants everyone at the company to believe Airbnb will be around for another century or more. If every company thought that way, we'd see very different business behavior. For example, it means you have to care about society, the environment, and stable government, because if those disintegrate, so will your business. If you're building technology, you have to think about what it might do 10 or 20 years out, and how it will impact the world. If you're creating new organisms by coding DNA, or developing lab-grown meat, or creating a new way to buy and sell art on a blockchain, an infinite time horizon makes you think, how could this go wrong, and how can we make sure it doesn't?

It's much easier to make decisions detrimental to society when the focus is on building valuation so you can sell the company in three years. Companies must be encouraged to always think in long time horizons.

SOLVE A PROBLEM, DON'T JUST MONETIZE IT

Every good company starts with a problem to solve. Amazon: Bookstores never have all the titles people want. YouTube:

There was no easy way to upload video to the internet so anyone could see it. Tesla: Electric cars are better for the environment but they suck. The difficulty comes when a company gets away from solving the problem and instead gets hooked on the revenue from repeatedly engaging users. That leads to unhealthy behavior like collecting data on users to find ways to manipulate them, as Facebook and YouTube do, or engineering foods so people eat more than they should, as snack food companies do.

Responsible companies ask, how do we solve the problem and then get out of the way? And how do we build a responsible business model that profits from disengagement rather than engagement?

A great disengagement dating app might only get paid when the user falls in love. (Presuming that's the problem the user wanted to solve when downloading the app!)

ELEVATE CONSIDERATION OF UNINTENDED CONSEQUENCES

When entrepreneurs are building a company, it's often overwhelming just trying to stay on top of day-to-day demands. But early in a company's existence, it's time to gather the leadership team, advisors, and board members and spend a day digging into questions like: What could go wrong? What if we succeed beyond our dreams?

When entrepreneurs are raising money, investors should insist on an in-depth analysis of unintended consequences. Founders should include these considerations in their pitch materials, and investors should dig deep into them during due diligence. Anticipating unintended consequences should assume as much significance as any other business metric when entrepreneurs and investors contemplate a partnership.

This seems like such a straightforward and obvious thing to do, but, in my experience, while founders and investors take the time to think about what could go wrong for the business (competition, regulation, etc.), they rarely think seriously about how the products they're building could do lasting damage if the business is a success.

BAKE THE CULTURE

Once a company has momentum, it's critical that the founder instill it with a culture that supports responsible innovation. Culture is like a decision-making compass for the workforce. It's one thing when the founder or CEO is making a decision guided by his or her conscience. But what about the thousands of daily decisions made by everyone else at the company? By making responsible innovation an explicit part of the culture, everyone will know to lean in that direction at all times.

Another element of culture is the way the outside world perceives the company—its brand, its image. I believe companies should be explicit about their intentions to be responsible, so that the branding relies on it. Taking actions that veer from that image would then cause the brand irreparable harm—a powerful motivator to do the right thing. So don't just keep your responsible innovation stance to yourself—tell the world and make the world expect it of you.

ORIENT GOVERNANCE AROUND MITIGATING UNINTENDED CONSEQUENCES

The mainstay of corporate governance is a board of directors that helps a business make important decisions and fulfill fiduciary responsibilities. Increasingly, many firms also have independent advisory boards to help address specific questions around tech development. In a similar vein, companies should consider creating board subcommittees or perhaps even independent bodies to govern how well they are managing unintended consequences. Doing so would ensure that unintended consequences are as important as other factors of good governance.

MEASURE THE RIGHT THINGS

Companies and investors have many ways to measure performance: revenue growth, earnings, valuation, stock price. Companies measure KPIs that might include net profit margin, operational cash flow, current accounts receivable, and inventory turnover. Yet such indicators are a measure of a business's financial success. They say nothing about whether the product is improving society or the lives of users—or making things worse.

Companies need a new set of measurements called KCIs, or key consequence indicators. There is no standard set of KCIs yet, though I expect that will change. This goes beyond today's ESG scores, which are also not standardized. In ESG, the environmental factors can include a company's energy use, waste, and pollution; social scores can look at a company's philanthropy, working conditions, and inclusiveness; governance might be about conflicts of interest, transparency, and political contributions. All of that can help a company know how well it's adhering to responsible innovation principles, but KCIs would score the *impact* of products and services. KCIs might show whether algorithms are biased, or users are appropriately engaged versus addicted. Each company might come up with its own set of KCIs based on its circumstances.

As Jennifer Howard-Grenville of the University of Cambridge wrote: "When Nike was critiqued for its suppliers' labor practices in the 1990s, for example, it took the time to interview 67,000 workers to explore the issues through their experiences, enabled by board member Jill Ker Conway's network of researchers and women's organizations. From this, the company was able to create a longer-term strategy involving disclosure, partnering with other brands to improve working conditions, and mobilizing community support. . . . Measures that capture *inputs* (such as the numbers of women on those teams) don't capture *outcomes* (such as decision-making that reflects diverse perspectives) and *impacts* (such as the social value created by such decisions) . . . which means that we have to look behind the numbers and ask how, why, and under what conditions they came about."[4]

BUILD ALGORITHMIC CANARIES

This is a powerful emerging concept in the world of AI. Essentially, companies need to develop AI that keeps an eye on its AI, watching for patterns that suggest an AI-driven product is veering off-path and causing harm. I'll dive deeper into this in the following chapter.

GROW ETHICALLY

In the world of tech startups, the dogma for nearly three decades has been that a company should grow as fast as possible, driven by the idea that the winner takes all in a digital economy. You want to be Uber, not Lyft; Google, not Bing. One highly popular book by LinkedIn founder Reid Hoffman was titled, *Blitzscaling: The Lightning-Fast Path to Building Massively Valuable Companies.*

But "blitz-scaling" can lead to irresponsible behaviors in the name of growth. It can be hard to foster a strong, responsible culture when hiring too many people too quickly. A breakneck pace certainly makes it more difficult to take time to reflect on what might go wrong.

Take the time to build a company that will endure, which means building a company that can avoid harmful unintended consequences. It's becoming apparent that in the future, companies that move too fast and cause harm will have a much more difficult time enduring.

IF YOU DISRUPT, ALSO REPAIR

Move fast and break things. Disrupt. Ready, fire, aim. Act now and ask for forgiveness later. It's time to retire these popular Silicon Valley adages.

It was once cool for tech startups to try to blow up incumbent industries and companies. But that's left an economy laden with displaced workers, created divisions in society, and stirred up political backlash. Amazon has shattered the traditional retail industry. Is society better off with shuttered storefronts everywhere? Craigslist devastated local newspapers by luring away classified ads (by making them free on its site). That's left most towns without strong local journalism, damaging those communities.[5]

Of course, some old ways of doing business deserve to be reinvented with technology. Certain jobs are going to get automated and displaced. But the lesson learned in the 2000s is that no company operates in a vacuum. Every company has to be responsible for maintaining a healthy ecosystem around it. This is what stakeholder capitalism is about: fostering a habitat that allows new companies to flourish and improve life.

For founders and leaders, that means partnering with incumbents instead of trying to destroy them. It means investing in retraining people so they can partake in the new economy you're inventing. Most important, it means being humble enough to know that your company exists only as long as society gives it permission to exist.

PARTNER WITH REGULATORS TO CREATE ACCOUNTABILITY

To manage unintended consequences, businesses must be open to sensible regulation that protects our collective interests.

We would benefit from innovators getting together to propose frameworks for self-regulation, though regulatory agencies may also play a useful role. The Food and Drug

Administration (FDA) is a good example of an agency that carefully considers the unintended medical harm a new drug or device may have before approving it for distribution. But even the FDA has blind spots when it comes to second- and third-order impacts on society as a whole. For instance, the FDA did not foresee that the approval of opioid painkillers would lead to a crisis of opioid addiction.

Innovators must help regulators see such next-order impacts in order to avoid longer-term unintended consequences.

MODEL THE FUTURE

One of the hardest things about preventing unintended consequences is that they are often very difficult to forecast. Lots of new technologies develop around your technology, possibly impacting how it's used or the effect it has. Societal norms shift. Policies change. New competitors arrive.

There's also a theory called the Collingridge Dilemma, coined by David Collingridge in his 1980 book *The Social Control of Technology*.[6] The Collingridge Dilemma goes like this: The impact of a technology can't be predicted until it is widely adopted; yet once a technology becomes widely adopted, it's difficult to change it. For instance, by the time it became clear that Amazon was going to damage vital community retail, there was no way to undo online commerce. If Collingridge is right, in some cases even algorithmic canary warnings or other alarms will come too late.

However, we're living in an era of big data, AI, and computer modeling. There are so many ways now to vacuum up all kinds of signals from social networks, e-commerce, and media, and these constant feedback loops can tell a company what's happening with its product at a granular level. Those signals can feed a computer model that could paint scenarios of what might happen if a certain trend continues.

I don't believe harmful consequences can't be predicted in time to avert them. I'm sure the Collingridge Dilemma was true in 1980. It's no longer true in the 2020s.

――――――

I run a venture capital firm, so I know VCs have an important role to play in responsible innovation.

We need to back up our intentions with investments. VCs have to believe responsible companies create more value over time and direct our investments to those companies.

We need to let founders know that every pitch deck must include a section on being responsible, with a clear indication of KCIs that will be tracked.

VCs often land on boards, so we are part of governance. We need to bring our responsible innovation mindset to governance and advocate for it inside companies.

In the past, VCs have been guilty of pumping too much money into startups and then pushing them to grow at breakneck speed. We must end that cycle, knowing that hypergrowth is a risk factor that can allow unintended consequences to happen, potentially bringing down the company.

VCs have also been guilty of liking "disruption" too much, without understanding that too much disruption damages the society that allows a company to exist and flourish. We need to be advocates of partnering, creating healthy ecosystems, and repairing what we damage.

Many VC firms have come around to this kind of thinking in the past few years. But it's not enough. For example, the Principles for Responsible Investment (PRI), a London-based organization partnered with the United Nations that oversees ESG commitments and practices of investors, as of late 2020 had more than 3,800 signatories covering every asset class from private equity to commodities and real estate. The total number of VC firms on the list, from all over the world, is just a few dozen, and almost none are among the largest firms.[7]

Venture-funded companies are often the companies that reinvent industries and change the way we live and work. If responsible innovation is going to take hold, the venture community has to take a leading role.

CHAPTER 8

ALGORITHMIC CANARIES

The Scottish Inverness Caledonian Thistle FC soccer club, more commonly known as Caley Thistle, plays in Scotland's second-tier league, in a stadium that holds a bit more than 7,000 people. This isn't a wealthy team, and it doesn't get much TV coverage. To give its fans more access to on-field action, the team bought a camera system from Pixellot, a company based in Israel.

Pixellot developed what it calls "AI-automated video." Mounted cameras around the field are driven by AI to follow the action, so no operators are needed, creating a broadcast-like experience while saving money. In soccer, Pixellot's AI is trained to follow the ball, which helps make sure the camera always frames the action.

Once deployed at Caley Thistle's stadium, the AI ran into an unintended consequence when the referee in a game was bald.[1] The AI couldn't tell the difference between a soccer ball and a bald head moving around the field. Pixellot told the press it could fix the problem with a tweak of the algorithm. And while mistaking a ball for a head didn't really do much damage other than make for some weird soccer viewing, the story shows how AI can go awry because its creators never considered a potential problem.

The ways AI can go wrong grow exponentially as it gets deployed in ever more complex ways. Consider language translation. AI is getting good at it, and already there are many AI translation tool companies, with Google leading the way with its service. There is no doubt AI can eventually obliterate language barriers. Encounter someone speaking a language you don't know, and you'll be able to hold up your phone, put in some earbuds, and listen to a simultaneous translation. But it's an enormously complex challenge.[2] These AIs are trained by ingesting hundreds of billions of words from sources that range from dictionaries to YouTube videos and chatter on Reddit. Google has an advantage here because it sees countless billions of searches, emails, and Google docs from around the world. The volume of data is so enormous, no human could know all of what's in it.

We're already seeing an unintended consequence that has ramifications for inequality. Some languages, including English, don't attach a gender to nouns. German, French, and some other languages do. When translating English to German or French, the AI must decide which gender to assign to an English noun. As a study by University of Cambridge researchers found, the translations tend toward stereotypes. A "cleaner" becomes feminine and an "engineer," masculine. The researchers found that the bias can be fixed by retraining the AI, but if such an AI were widely used before the problem was noticed, it could have caused hurtful consequences.

A botched soccer video or a biased language translator are relatively mild consequences when you realize that AI is this era's electricity—it's eventually going to power just about everything. An AI's creators can be diverse, have the best intentions, and try to be diligent, yet they will inevitably miss something. Imagine the potential damage if an AI guiding someone's healthcare goes wrong, or if an AI operating a dam or helping weapons identify targets has a glitch.

Companies dedicated to responsible innovation need to make sure their AI doesn't lead to unintended consequences. Their business model mechanisms may do a great job supporting good intentions, but if the AI has built-in, unseen biases or flaws, bad things can happen anyway.

As the use of AI grows, so does the potential for unintended consequences. In early 2021, the US Federal Trade Commission warned businesses and health systems that discriminatory algorithms could violate consumer protection laws. "Hold yourself accountable—or be ready for the FTC to do it for you," Elisa Jillson, an attorney in the FTC's privacy and identity protection division, wrote in an official blog post.[3] The FTC prohibits unfair or deceptive practices, which could include the use of racially biased algorithms, Jillson wrote. In 2019, Congress introduced a bill, the Algorithmic Accountability Act, that would direct the FTC to develop regulations requiring large firms to conduct impact assessments for existing and new "high-risk automated decision systems"—in other words, AI.[4] The European Union in the summer of 2021 was considering strict AI accountability rules. None of these proposals have yet been passed into law, but it's obvious that companies must act quickly and responsibly or they will face regulation.

Yet companies aren't doing enough. In the spring of 2021, Boston Consulting Group released a report noting that more than half of enterprises overestimate the capabilities of their efforts to responsibly use AI, while just 12 percent have even fully implemented a responsible AI program.[5]

Businesses need a reliable approach to avoid unintended consequences of AI—a tech mechanism that works alongside the business model to support and ensure a company's responsible mindset.

I call such an approach "algorithmic canaries."

———

Like the proverbial canary in a coal mine, an algorithmic canary provides a warning that gives a company a chance to stop a disaster before it happens. It is AI built specifically to watch another AI—a software sentry that can do what humans could never do by watching billions of data points and looking for patterns that suggest something is amiss. Startups need to put these canaries in place to make sure their AI is tracking with the company's intentions and sound an alarm if the technology is causing harm, or if others are hijacking the AI and using it in a harmful way (à la foreigners taking advantage of Facebook's algorithm to influence elections). An AI canary can also keep an eye on all of a company's business practices to help it stay responsible.

The technology to do this can be built. One example is the Allen Institute's Grover, an algorithm that can find "fake news" generated by AI among real news reports and block it before it reaches a mass audience. In a machine version of "it takes one to know one," a Brookings Institution study found that since AI generates fake news, AI can also get familiar with the kind of quirks and traits an AI news story displays. The study concluded that Grover was 92 percent accurate at detecting human- versus machine-written news.

A variety of companies already build AI that can collect billions of data points and look for patterns that predict problems. Noodle.ai, for instance, developed AI that can monitor signals from machines in a factory, trucks along the supply chain, changes in weather, and even news reports to predict what might go wrong in a manufacturer's operations from raw material to shelf, so the manufacturer can keep everything flowing smoothly. New York–based Sprinklr builds AI that captures signals from a company's customers everywhere they might be chatting—Twitter, chatbots, reviews, emails, calls to customer service—to help the company spot and fix a problem with its product or brand before it gets worse.

A UK company, Signal AI, offers AI that can monitor many aspects of a business, among them its ESG performance. "Understanding your business, supply chain, clients, partners, whether they are representing values and attributes expected as part of ESG, or trends that suggest a breach of that—it's becoming quite viable and possible with AI," says Signal AI CEO David Benigson.[6]

If AI can already do all of those things, we can develop AI that can watch another AI for biases or bad actions.

At the same time, a new flavor of AI, dubbed "explainable AI," is an effort to build AI that is less of an indecipherable black box and more easily watched and tuned by its operators.

Jeff Hawkins—creator of the Palm Pilot, brain researcher, and founder of Numenta—is developing AI that works more like the human brain. "When we build brain-like AI, it will be less of a black box because it will have more structure in it and we'll know what its pieces are doing," Hawkins says. "We'll have a better ability to look inside and know why it did what it did."[7]

So, the problem isn't that it's too hard to build an AI that can watch another AI and sound an alarm if something is amiss. The challenge is identifying what the AI canary should be looking for.

We need these AIs to anticipate unintended consequences, like when the business vacuums up data to be monetized through advertising. AIs also need to identify second- or third-order consequences, such as what happens to a city when e-commerce forces numerous retail stores to close.

Ultimately, while the types of unintended consequences will vary company by company, the industry must begin to develop a collective approach to what algorithmic canaries should guard against. This requires understanding all the stakeholders the company touches.

ESG is a useful starting point. It encourages companies to think of unintended consequences across environmental, social, and governance issues. But algorithmic canaries need to go much further. Such AIs should look for consequences such as misinformation campaigns, privacy intrusions, inequality, social isolation, and racial discrimination.

The best practice would be for founders to incorporate algorithmic canaries at the early stage of product development—bake it into the product and business. If you're doing this retroactively, it's probably too late. Taking a systems design approach to responsibility and clearly articulating and measuring it allows engineering teams to embed canaries deeply into their technologies and track them as KCIs. In this way, companies can begin to measure what really matters beyond their own success: the potential unintended consequences of their technologies and their leaders' responsibility to mitigate them.

———

While companies need to build algorithmic canaries into their products, I believe society also needs the government to play a role. In fact, the United States needs what might be called a Federal Artificial Intelligence Agency, or FAIA. And it probably needs to build algorithmic canaries to watch other algorithmic canaries.

First, though, we need an FAIA staffed with AI experts because we don't elect people because they're experts in AI. We elect them because (we hope!) they are experts at governing. In the past, to help our officials manage an important emerging technology, the government has set up some sort of agency to provide expertise and oversight. For instance, World War II unleashed the ability to split atoms—a technology that created nuclear bombs but also had the potential for nuclear energy. (There were even ideas at the time that atomic energy could be used to propel rockets and make your garden grow.) In 1946, Congress passed the Atomic Energy Act establishing the Atomic Energy Commission, which later evolved into the current Nuclear Regulatory Commission (NRC).[8]

Now, the NRC also reveals the catch in government oversight. We don't want overreaching regulation that goes beyond keeping us safe and ends up stifling innovation. Regulators helped make it so difficult to develop atomic energy that the United States gets only 20 percent of its electricity from nuclear power. (France gets 70 percent.)[9]

While we need an FAIA, I would prefer to see it created as a public-private partnership. Washington should bring in AI experts from the tech industry to a federal agency designed to understand and direct AI and to inform lawmakers. Perhaps the AI experts would rotate through Washington on a kind of public service tour of duty.

We're likely at the beginning of a new era in government—one where more governance happens in software. Old-school regulations that rely on manual enforcement are too cumbersome to keep up with technology and too "dumb" to monitor algorithms in a timely way. Software-defined regulation can monitor software-driven industries better than regulations enforced by squads of regulators. If Congress wants to make sure Facebook doesn't exploit political biases, it could direct the FAIA to write an algorithm to look for that.

It's just as important to have algorithms that keep an eye on the role of humans inside these companies. We want tech that can tell if Airbnb hosts are illegally turning down minorities or if Facebook's human editors are squashing conservative news headlines. The watchdog algorithms can be like open-source software—open to examination by anyone, while the companies keep private proprietary algorithms and data. If the algorithms are public, anyone can run various data sets against them and analyze for "off the rails" behaviors and unexpected results.

Tech companies and policy makers need to come together soon and share ideas about AI governance and establishing a software-driven AI agency. The Institute of Electrical and Electronics Engineers (IEEE), the powerful engineering society, is working on guidelines it calls Algorithmic Bias Considerations to help with the "ethical alignment in intelligent and autonomous systems." The resources are available. The industry stands ready.[10]

We have a chance to tee up AI so it does tremendous good. But to unleash it in a positive direction, we need to get the checks and balances in place right now.

CHAPTER 9

ETHICAL GROWTH

The way founders must think about optimal growth rate can be examined through a tale of two companies providing businesses with cloud-based software for payroll, benefits, and human resource management. Gusto was started in 2011 by founder and CEO Joshua Reeves. My firm became an investor. Zenefits was founded in 2013 by Parker Conrad. Investors included several high-profile venture firms.

By 2015, Zenefits was getting all the attention. That spring, its valuation jumped to $4.5 billion, up from $500 million the previous year. From 2014 to 2015, it grew from $1 million in annual recurring revenue to $20 million. The company set a goal of hitting $100 million in revenue in 2016. It signed up about 10,000 small businesses as customers and hired like crazy to keep up with demand. The press gave it breathless write-ups. According to a story in *Forbes*, "Zenefits was already the hottest startup of 2014. Now it's making a case to grab the same title in 2015."[1]

The poison that would soon cripple Zenefits was buried in that *Forbes* story. The writer pointed out that Zenefits was growing so fast because it made its software free to businesses, and then made money on commissions from health insurers and other providers on benefits sold to its customers. So, to make money and keep up the pace of growth, Zenefits' employees were under intense pressure to push products on its customers—often products the customers might not want or need. And Conrad kept intensifying that pressure in an attempt to overtake all competitors and own the market. He said his investors "agree that we should be stepping on the gas and pushing the pedal to the floor. We're trying to get as much of the market as we can."[2]

The pressure to grow led to cutting corners to get around regulations that would've slowed the company. Zenefits soon found it was being scrutinized by regulators for letting brokers sell health insurance in states where they weren't licensed, leading to nearly $9 million in fines. The company wrote internal software that let its brokers spend fewer hours in online training than was required by California law. Conrad later admitted that Zenefits' engineering capabilities couldn't keep up with demands, leading to errors when employees tried to do things manually. As problems grew, growth stalled. The Securities and Exchange Commission brought charges of misleading investors.

Conrad resigned in early 2016. "I was hiding at home, like, kind of borderline suicidal and not talking to anyone and watching this disaster unfold around me," he told a journalist.[3] The company's valuation was cut in half and it laid off nearly half its employees as it recast its business model. Now it sells the software as a subscription instead of relying on brokerage commissions.

As Gusto watched Zenefits go through its drama, Reeves kept his focus on responsible, optimal growth. It wasn't always easy seeing Zenefits get so much attention, but by sticking to its mechanisms that support its mindset of helping small companies grow, Gusto eventually came out ahead. "We want to earn the right to be around for decades," Reeves says, echoing the concept of using long time horizons to keep a company's behavior in check.[4]

Gusto didn't reject growth—it rejected irresponsible growth. "Silicon Valley views have been too binary: do we blitz-scale or not?" Reeves says. "Is it bad to think we should grow as fast as we can? No, it's not bad at all. But a good reason to grow is if there is a large amount of customer pain to solve for as many people as possible, not to make as much money as possible faster."

Optimal, responsible growth starts with the right business model. From the beginning, Gusto sold its service as a subscription. Since customers had to pay for it, Gusto didn't get the fast uptake Zenefits did by making its service free. But the model avoided Zenefits' pitfalls and meant Gusto's customers had to get value from the service, or they would cancel.

Reeves also instituted what he calls three checks and balances on growth. The first was customer experience. Gusto developed metrics to track whether it was solving customers' problems or creating more. Of course, if Gusto ever starts causing problems, that's a signal to slow down and get it right. And if the metrics show customers are too pleased, Reeves takes it as a sign that Gusto might be growing too conservatively.

The second check was around employee experience. Gusto does regular employee surveys and keeps tabs on

churn and morale. If people feel burned out or wouldn't recommend working at Gusto, or if employees stay for a few
months and quit, those are signs that growth is getting ahead
of the ability to manage the company well. On the other
hand, if employees feel like their jobs are a walk in the park,
they're probably not being pushed hard enough to help the
company grow.

Finally, Gusto measured the performance of its business model as a way to calibrate growth rate. For instance, it
watches how much it spends to acquire customers and how
much it spends to serve them. If the company has negative
gross margin and is counting on the next funding round to
refill that leaky bucket, the growth rate is probably not sustainable. Time to slow down and get it right. However, if the
metrics are too comfortable, the company is likely not spending enough resources on growth.

How has Gusto's approach to growth worked out? Really
well. The company's last round of funding, in 2021, valued it at
$9.5 billion. It serves more than 100,000 small businesses with
software that manages payroll, health insurance, HR, and
more. It also has 1,000 employees, 65 percent of whom would
recommend Gusto as a place to work, according to Glassdoor,
while 85 percent approve of CEO Reeves. In turn, Reeves says,
"We will be a multidecade independent business."

Zenefits is still in the game, but it lost a lot of ground. New
CEO Jay Fulcher told the *San Francisco Chronicle*: "It's really
important to recognize that growth at all cost or at any cost is
not a good idea."[5]

I want to be clear: Growth is good. Growth should be the goal of any company. But hypergrowth, or blitz-scaling, for the wrong reasons is irresponsible and potentially harmful. Wrong reasons include using growth as a way to "win" a market, as a path to cashing out for a lot of money, or because investors pumped the company full of excess capital that the company is then expected to spend on growth.

From the dawn of the dot-com boom in 1995 and through 2020, "responsible growth" might have seemed like an oxymoron in Silicon Valley. The tech startup ecosystem was more likely to celebrate any means of growth. Hypergrowth made headlines and hypnotized investors. But now some of the reasons for that attitude look like myths.

One of those myths is that we're in a winner-take-all economy, so that in every market category, one company is going to run away with 75 percent-plus of the economics and everyone else will get the scraps. That may have been true 20 or even 10 years ago, when a lot of startups were network-effect companies, which meant everyone would want to belong to the biggest network. These are companies like Facebook, LinkedIn, Twitter—or companies like Google, where as more people use it, the better its algorithms get at search, which in turn convinces more people to use it . . . and the flywheel keeps spinning faster, leaving competitors behind.

But today, many startups are reinventing big, longstanding industries that impact everyday life—industries like insurance, healthcare, energy, banking, and shipping. The same network effects don't play out. These markets are enormous. Look at Gusto: it's built a multibillion-dollar business by serving 100,000 small companies in a market where there are millions of small companies yet to be touched by it. Tesla isn't going to make all the electric cars in the world. Teledoc isn't going to replace all in-person doctor visits by offering them virtually. In these kinds of industries, market domination is almost impossible. Instead, companies should focus on aggressive but manageable growth rates over a long period of time.

Another myth has been "first mover advantage"—the idea that being first to introduce a new technology or business model confers an enormous lead over those who follow you. That mentality is used to justify irresponsible tactics like "move fast and break things." But that myth has been exploded by the many first movers that have tanked while latecomers succeeded. Google wasn't the first search engine. AWS wasn't the first cloud computing platform. Netflix wasn't the first streaming video service.

Silicon Valley has been obsessed with this idea of backing the hacker-entrepreneur who moves fast, puts out a least viable product, and iterates. But that is not well suited to building responsibly.

What can confuse people is that sometimes irresponsible innovation works. It most famously worked for Uber. The company's caustic culture celebrated breaking rules and behaving badly. Instead of working with cities, it stormed into them and later asked for forgiveness, counting on policy makers to be too scared to take away a service that consumers liked. But operating that way is a gamble. Uber got lucky, though it has faced major challenges from cities like London and New York. But more often, the gambler loses.

We should be celebrating the empathetic entrepreneur who understands customer needs deeply and figures out the responsible way to serve them, even if it comes at the expense of some growth. Such companies, like Gusto, plan to be around for decades, and they set up a business model, culture, and governance with that goal in mind—then monitor metrics to make sure the company stays on track.

There is an optimal growth rate unique to each company. What is the pace of hiring required to service the next market segment, and can the company get the right employees and properly train them? How complex are the logistics of delivering new services? Such questions help figure out a growth plan that makes sense.

Other companies I've been involved with have scaled responsibly and aggressively. One is Stripe, the online payments company that has become the commerce backbone for the tech startup ecosystem. Providing a global online payments application programming interface (API) was a massive opportunity. Stripe took it in steps, building from its core. It wanted to first get the majority of newly founded companies to sign up for their commerce capabilities. That ensured Stripe's future. Then it started to go upmarket to also serve companies that have been around for a while.[6]

Another right-scaled company is Livongo. Its objective is to keep consumers with diabetes healthy. Those consumers have many comorbidities, like hypertension and obesity, and Livongo realized it needed to deepen its offering much sooner to address those conditions because it was the right thing to do for its customers. In general, the decisions about how fast to scale and why are different for every company.

It's important to acknowledge, too, that outside forces impact growth and must be managed. Something I hear from every founder who wants to build responsibly is that it's vitally important to choose the right investors and board, making sure they share the same mindset. The wrong investors will focus on the short term, pushing for fast growth and a quick return on investment. The right investors will want to be partners for the long haul, building a company that matters and lasts for generations.

Yet, as important as it is, choosing the right investors and board isn't enough. It's up to the founder to constantly reinforce the message of responsible growth, conditioning investors and all stakeholders to embrace such a philosophy, and doing it over and over again. The best CEOs leave no question about their stance. They want to build an enduring company that benefits society and stakeholders alike.

CHAPTER 10

CULTURE AND GOVERNANCE

A company's *culture* is the keeper of its mindset. It's how a company infuses its responsible innovation ethos into every employee and stakeholder—and pushes away those who don't buy into that ethos.

A company's *governance* is the protector of its mechanisms. The board must understand how the business model, algorithmic canaries, and relevant metrics support the mindset, and then defend those elements when they come under pressure.

And so it follows that any leadership team determined to practice responsible innovation has to be intentional and thoughtful about culture and governance.

Culture typically comes first—best when developed early in a company's life. "Culture is a company's instinct," says Zach Reitano, CEO of Ro, which provides online healthcare and medication. "It's what people do when no one is watching; when there's not an executive in the room."[1]

In October 2017, Reitano, Saman Rahmanian, and Rob Schutz founded what was then called Roman. The idea for the company came from a personal insight. As a young man,

Reitano had a heart condition that led to erectile dysfunction (ED). He became acquainted with the indignities and barriers that men faced when needing ED medications. A lot of insurers don't cover ED medications, and a dozen pills could cost hundreds of dollars. Many men feel embarrassed talking about the problem face-to-face with a physician and want to avoid waiting in a drugstore where a clerk might announce: "Mr. So-and-so, please pick up your Viagra." Initially, Ro was launched just for ED. The site let men talk to or email a doctor online, and set up a monthly subscription to get the pills by mail, at a cost far less than at pharmacies.

In part because of Reitano's experience, Ro started life with extreme empathy for its users and made that empathy the centerpiece of its culture, even as the company expanded into services for women and set a goal to be an "end-to-end healthcare experience from diagnosis, to delivery of medication, to ongoing care," as its website declares.

"Our philosophy has always been, we treat patients for life," Reitano says. "We don't believe that there is a difference, long term, between what's best for the business and best for the patient. If we do what's best for patients we'll build a sustainable business. When there's a conflict that might hurt short-term revenue, we show people externally and internally that we have a long-term outlook and will do what's responsible for the long term."

Ro in 2021 had around 400 employees. When it was still just 15 people a few years before, the group sat down to write out the core company values. It came up with five words: *relentless* (we work hard); *effective* (we work effectively); *empathetic* (toward patients and each other); *curiosity* (when something goes wrong, ask why); and *magic* (going the extra mile to do something great). Empathy and curiosity, in particular, go a long way toward keeping the company on a path of responsible innovation. Everyone in the company understands that the five values plus the umbrella concept of treating patients for life form the heart and soul of Ro's culture.

How does Ro keep that culture alive year after year? The five values are baked into performance reviews. Every two weeks, the leadership team has an all-hands meeting where it gives shout-outs to employees who did something exemplary around one or more of the values. And in their day-to-day interactions, the founders consistently refer to the values and make decisions based on them.

Reitano believes the culture informs responsible decision-making deep in the company. Here's just a small example of how that works: Ro always sends patients an automated email 24 hours before shipping to make sure the person actually wants what's coming. That gives the patient a way to click and say no, don't send it, and don't charge me. At one point, though, a bug in the system turned that function off, so patients didn't have a chance to say no. As you might guess, the bug increased retention. Without having an option, more patients just accepted the shipment, boosting Ro's revenues.

A lot of companies might see that as fortuitous. They might say: "Great, let's stop sending that email! Better for the bottom line!" But when employees at Ro found the bug, they knew what to do: they turned the function back on. They knew that patient trust is more important in the long run than a bump in revenues. "The second patients get an inclination you're not acting in their best interests, they'll leave you forever," Reitano says. "No $20 is worth the lifetime value of a patient. We make sure we live by those principles."

Ro secured a $500 million round of funding in March 2021 that valued the company at $5 billion. It's becoming one of the most recognized brands in online healthcare and is likely to be a significant player in healthcare for years to come. It's showing that a culture built around responsible innovation works.

Compared to Ro, Ginkgo Bioworks has an even greater need to build a responsible innovation culture. Ginkgo was founded in 2009 by CEO Jason Kelly and a group of genetic engineering scientists from MIT. Basically, Ginkgo is building tools that can let people program the DNA of cells the way they program computers. That creates an ability to design custom organisms, which means, for instance, that a company could use Ginkgo to program cells to grow meat more efficiently, or create new kinds of antibiotics that defeat resistant bacteria, or grow high-powered biofuels. Ginkgo bills itself as a platform for bioengineering, much as Amazon's AWS is a platform for cloud computing.

But, bioengineering could lead to dangerous unintended consequences, whether by mistake or by design. (It's not hard to imagine some Bond villain making a microbe that would quickly replicate and poison a city's drinking water unless a ransom is paid.) "Because biology is so potent, we have got to be careful," Kelly says.[2]

Ginkgo's culture is its first line of defense against unintended consequences. "We have this tenet: we care how our platform is used," Kelly says. "Silicon Valley has this concept of, my platform is a tool and I'm not responsible for how it's used. But we have to care."

When a new use case comes up, an internal committee digs into it and tries to look ahead at potential consequences, which includes societal risk as well as regulatory and legal risks for the company. Kelly says he wants to bring in people who could be affected by a new bioengineered product to be part of those committees, helping Ginkgo avoid what Kelly calls "blind spots." Maybe military veterans who lived through the use of Agent Orange should help identify the potential consequences of a new microbe for use in battle. "The hard part is seeing around corners—how the platform could be misused," Kelly says. Trying to do that is the job of Ginkgo's culture, and everyone at Ginkgo plays a role.

An important piece of that is employee ownership. Ginkgo has about 600 employees and most have a stake in the company. "That helps make our people care how the platform is used," Kelly says. "It ups the odds they'll see around corners." And Kelly's team encourages employees to speak up if they spot potential trouble or have concerns.

To raise issues the company needs to consider, Ginkgo also makes use of an interesting mechanism: an online magazine called *Grow*. Recent stories have included a discussion of scientific uncertainty and a thoughtful piece about efforts to end aging. "As a platform to engineer life, we have interesting and challenging ethical components," says *Grow*'s editor, Christina Agapakis. "*Grow* is a forcing function for our own thinking. We put in our point of view and bring in other thinkers, and it guides us when thinking through hard issues."[3]

Grow is also part of an external cultural strategy focused on the emerging culture of cell programmers. "We can have a disproportionate impact on that culture," CEO Kelly says. "We need to be intentional about what it means to be a cell programmer." It's like infusing doctors with the culture of "first, do no harm" or airline pilots with an extreme "safety first" mentality.

In any company, culture is hard to change once it gets baked—but not impossible. Uber eased away from its hard-charging, corner-cutting culture once its founders left and it became obvious that Uber's old culture was damaging the company. The new leadership at Zenefits is trying to change its culture in part by changing the business model and instituting entirely different objectives for employees. And yet, in both cases, I believe the companies would be better off today if they had built responsible innovation into their cultures from the beginning.

Of course, culture is a mushy topic. Every company's culture is different, and cultures form in different ways. But culture is heavily informed by the founders, and the main point here is that founders who want to operate responsibly must understand that culture is a key lever. Treat it as such. Be intentional about developing a culture that is concerned with responsible innovation and unintended consequences. Make every person in the company care how the product gets used and about its impact, and give them a way to sound alarms.

How else might a leadership team think about culture?

- Align the culture with your responsible innovation ethos. For instance, make sure every employee knows what your KCIs are, and make employees as responsible for those metrics as they are for performance metrics. Give employees the power to act to preserve the company's responsible ethos and to be heard when they identify a potentially harmful consequence.

- Develop a culture of radical collaboration. Explicitly seek diversity of thought so that the organization learns from it and it informs everything the company does.

- Encourage a culture of endurance. Like Airbnb, Corning, and Guild Education, build a culture that feels bigger than the people in it, guided by the idea that the company must be around for generations. Such a mindset helps assure that the culture will act like radar for long-term consequences, seeing dangers while they can be addressed.

- Acknowledge that there's a healthy tension between short-term tactics and long-term goals. Develop a culture that always weighs the two against each other before making a decision or taking an action.

- Identify people you may need to bring in or positions you may need to create to help solidify and tend to the culture. For example, when Twilio, a cloud communications platform, wanted to deepen its culture of responsible innovation, it created a new position of "VP of Ethical Use" and installed its general counsel, Mark Kahn, in the role.

In general, understand that culture helps the company and its people navigate ambiguity. It guides behavior in much the same way as religion, giving employees a moral resource to fall back on. That sensibility can help the company develop the right kinds of products, hire the right kinds of people, and treat stakeholders in ways that uphold and strengthen the company's mindset and mechanisms.

Creating a culture is a highly nuanced process. It's very personal to each founder and company. Governance is more straightforward.

Companies guided by responsible innovation principles should want governance that supports that ethos and helps make sure the leadership team adheres to it. Here are a few factors to consider when setting up a company's governance:

- First and foremost, you want board members who believe in responsible innovation and an infinite time horizon. Beyond that, seek diversity of thought so the board can help see potential unintended consequences across the breadth of society.
- If you don't go as far as creating a responsible innovation committee on the board, at least make sure the board has a responsible innovation agenda and pays as much attention to KCIs as it does to KPIs.
- Make sure classes of stock aren't set up to give the founder overwhelming control. Over the past two decades, there's been a trend in Silicon Valley of founders trying to control governance by hoarding voting shares. That sometimes makes sense, but if a company truly has an infinite time horizon, then it is bigger than the founder, and the founder needs to be held accountable if he or she veers from the

company's ethical path. Founders need to maintain the power they need to drive the company, yet build in accountability for themselves.

- Finally, understand that governance is a way to establish checks and balances. It should be aligned with the culture, but also a counterweight to the culture—there to insert itself if the culture or leadership strays from responsible innovation principles.

Creating the right culture and governance is one of the most important roles a founder can play. Company cultures have always flowed from the mindset and actions of their founders. To keep a company on a responsible innovation path, a key duty of the leadership team is to create and support a culture anchored in responsible innovation.

CHAPTER 11

STEWARDSHIP AND ANTITRUST

For the past few decades, the ultimate goal for a venture capitalist or founder has been to create a monopoly.

And you can see why: Today's big technology monopolies—Google in search; Apple with its iPhone; Facebook in social networking; Amazon in online retail—are all trillion-dollar companies. Even past tech companies with monopoly power were formidable, including Microsoft, IBM, the old AT&T, and, for a while, AOL. (Microsoft, IBM, and AT&T were prosecuted for antitrust violations.)

In an era of responsible innovation, the monopoly objective needs to change. Monopolies are corrosive for the economy and dangerous for society. We must create a new direction for antitrust and competition policy, aimed not just at protecting consumers from high prices but at protecting innovation and resilience. And we need a new attitude among investors and founders that I call "benevolent stewardship"—the idea that responsible companies shouldn't seek to own a market but instead seek to lead the growth of an ecosystem.

I don't have to make a case against unchecked technology monopolies because Congress made it very well in a 2020 document, "Investigation of Competition in Digital Markets." In the opening section, pointing to Google, Apple, Facebook, and Amazon, the report reads:

> Although these four corporations differ in important ways, studying their business practices has revealed common problems. First, each platform now serves as a gatekeeper over a key channel of distribution. By controlling access to markets, these giants can pick winners and losers throughout our economy.
>
> They not only wield tremendous power, but they also abuse it by charging exorbitant fees, imposing oppressive contract terms, and extracting valuable data from the people and businesses that rely on them. Second, each platform uses its gatekeeper position to maintain its market power.
>
> By controlling the infrastructure of the digital age, they have surveilled other businesses to identify potential rivals, and have ultimately bought out, copied, or cut off their competitive threats.
>
> And, finally, these firms have abused their role as intermediaries to further entrench and expand their dominance. Whether through self-preferencing, predatory pricing, or exclusionary conduct, the dominant platforms have exploited their power in order to become even more dominant.
>
> Although these firms have delivered clear benefits to society, the dominance of Amazon, Apple, Facebook,

and Google has come at a price. The Subcommittee's series of hearings produced significant evidence that these firms wield their dominance in ways that erode entrepreneurship, degrade Americans' privacy online, and undermine the vibrancy of the free and diverse press. The result is less innovation, fewer choices for consumers, and a weakened democracy.[1]

Even if you disagree with some parts of the report, that's a pretty damning picture.

In the United States, antitrust law is failing us. The Sherman Act and Clayton Act, passed during the era of massive trusts in the late nineteenth and early twentieth centuries, were intended to protect consumers from abusive monopolies. Over time, courts decided that the purpose of the laws was more narrow: to prevent monopolies from raising prices on consumers. That poses a problem today. The tech giants give consumers outstanding products for free (think Google Maps or Facebook Messenger) and often force prices down (as Amazon has done by underpricing traditional retailers). And current law generally does not prohibit "innocent monopolies" that win just by being great at what they do. Instead it targets monopolists who intentionally and nefariously squash competition. For the most part, our tech giants seem to have won their monopolies by playing by existing rules better than anyone. That's not breaking laws. In fact, if the companies' main concern is increasing shareholder value, economist Milton Friedman style, then behaving this way is what they should do.

Enforcement under existing antitrust law also relies heavily on defining a "market" that is dominated or monopolized by the alleged bad actor. The problem now is that dominant tech companies don't look like the oil and steel monopolies of the past. Increasingly, tech companies are giant, generalized software factories. They dominate one segment of a market (such as smartphones, search engines, or social media) and leverage the advantages of that segment (massive capital, distribution, and data, along with the ability to compete for the world's best technology talent) into dominance in other areas like email, mapping, productivity software, virtual reality headsets, streaming video, groceries—you name it. This kind of market dominance doesn't eliminate all competition, but it makes it dramatically harder to develop major competitors unless they are also giant generalized-software factories. The talent, data, and capital advantages are just too large. As a result, Google, Apple, Facebook, and Amazon dominate multiple markets and increasingly move into new ones, yet are largely unchallenged by antitrust regulators.

While this may change with different enforcement priorities in the US Department of Justice, it's unlikely to do so in a major way without a change in law. Unless we reimagine the whole concept of monopoly and market dominance, and the way we define markets for these kinds of businesses, the problem is going to get worse.

The dangers of technology monopolies are different from past industrial monopolies. As Congress pointed out, technology monopolies erode entrepreneurship. The power of Amazon discourages new retail. Apple demands a 30 percent cut of anything sold through its app store, making it more daunting to build a new mobile app company. Facebook sees a potential competing product (like Snap) and tries to copy it and steal the competitor's users. By every measure, business creation is falling. The rate of Americans deciding to become entrepreneurs has been steadily decreasing, according to the Kauffman Foundation. The Brookings Institution found that since 2008, firm creation rates have been below business death rates—the first time that's happened since the data began to be collected in the 1970s.[2] Since innovation and entrepreneurship are the greatest drivers of the American economy, we all stand to lose if that gets squashed.

Here's another problem with some of our technology monopolies: they are a massive potential breaking point for the entire national economy. Just imagine if something took down Google—a cyberattack, maybe, or some enormous financial collapse. All those personal and business Gmail accounts would go dark; Android phones wouldn't work; in search, we'd all have to figure out if Bing still exists. Google has become such a necessity, it could be considered a utility, like a power or water company—protected and regulated to ensure it stays operational. As an unregulated monopoly, it's risky to trust Google with such power. (In June 2021, Ohio Attorney General Dave Yost filed a lawsuit asking a court to declare Google a public utility that should be regulated. As of this writing, the suit is not resolved.[3])

Then what do we do? Just telling founders "Don't be a monopoly" isn't likely to be effective. Governments will have to curb existing tech monopolies and discourage new ones—but we don't want that to be too heavy-handed. Too much government regulation leads to less innovation. (The European Union has approached regulating technology power by trying to anticipate where technology is likely to go over the next decade or so, and then building a comprehensive legislative system to cover it. Such an approach, however, seldom hits the target and inevitably produces a range of unintended consequences, including stifled innovation.)

In addition to focusing on protecting consumers, I believe policy makers and regulators must focus on protecting small companies from unfair competition. That may mean changing antitrust laws so they take into account damage to small companies, and forcing the giants to divest some of their businesses to reduce their power. Amazon the retailer should probably separate from AWS the cloud-hosting service. Facebook the social network should not be allowed to own Instagram and WhatsApp.

It may also mean putting in place a series of legislative requirements for very large companies that treat them more like utilities or encourage competition. This could include mandatory data portability, so that users can easily take their data to competitors. It could also include policies that ensure what I call "platform responsibility." Amazon, Facebook, the iPhone, and Google are all platforms. A typical platform has access to customers, runs on proprietary algorithms, and owns the floods of data that come in from the platform's usage. Amazon, for instance, has a relationship with hundreds of millions of customers; sucks in data about purchases, products, and customer preferences; and has its own algorithms that learn from all that data to make Amazon's offerings even more competitive. When other retailers sell on Amazon's platform, they get access to Amazon's customers, but not the data or algorithms, leaving those retailers at a distinct disadvantage. Amazon can use the data to see a retail trend, hop on it, and put smaller competitors out of business.

One solution would be to develop laws that force platform owners to open at least two of those three elements—customers, data, or algorithms—to other companies that operate on the platform. That would help create a healthier ecosystem, which ultimately is good for the platform owner, while diminishing the power of the platform owner. We need innovation protection.

Stimulating innovation would create more competition, which is better for consumers. And diminishing the power of monopolies while creating more competition adds to the resilience of the economy. No one company becomes too big to fail.

Finally, in a previous chapter I described how companies should deploy algorithmic canaries to keep an eye on AI products and services, watching for misuse or dangerous consequences and sounding an alarm. Governments also need to deploy their own algorithmic canaries that watch for anticompetitive, anti-innovation monopolistic practices. Technology moves too fast for humans to monitor. After-the-fact investigations take too long, and by the time action is taken, the damage is done. The Justice Department prosecuted Microsoft in 2001, long after it had killed off competitors like Netscape.

Don't get me wrong: I would rather avoid regulatory solutions to monopolistic power. I want rules that discourage monopolies so responsible innovation ecosystems can flourish. Those ecosystems will spin out new technologies and companies that improve life, make the economy resilient, and give consumers more goods and services for less money.

As a new generation of companies become the new platforms, they must operate responsibly and build their ecosystems, not drive toward a monopoly. That's the essence of benevolent stewardship. Lots of founders want to create a new platform—becoming a significant platform is usually a big win. But the new platform owners must think about their businesses in a more responsible way.

When a company gets into the business of building a platform, it needs to think about platform governance, which refers to a company's decisions, policies, and processes determining who can use its platform.

The first step is to have a policy. The worst mistake is to have no policy and have to make one up each time something bad happens. It doesn't matter what kind of platform you're building—any kind of platform can be misused. A platform by definition lets other people or companies do things on it. YouTube lets others post videos. Salesforce.com lets developers build services on top. Stripe's platform can be used to process payments by any app or website. AWS can provide cloud computing to any entity. So what is YouTube going to do when terrorists post recruiting videos? What will Stripe do if a White supremacist site wants to use it to process payments for racist merchandise? What if a pornography business sets up on AWS? These can be tough calls. Most companies are deeply uneasy about being arbiters of truth and morality, but recognize that they have a responsibility to avoid amplifying and fueling harmful activity.

To deal with these many challenges, companies must increasingly think deeply about platform governance well *before* problems surface. I suggest gathering the leadership team and hammering out a policy, writing it down, and using it as a guide. To get started, here are some questions companies need to ask themselves:

- How can our platform be misused? What incentives are we creating (or that others can create using our platform) that might lead to bad behavior? Can we systematically reduce those incentives?
- Where do we sit in the stack? For example, are we basic infrastructure, a higher-level application, or a consumer-facing website? Generally speaking, the closer a service sits to individual users and the more visibility it has into their behavior, the more the responsibility sits with that service to control how it is used.
- What is the magnitude of harm we will be conscious of, and what evidence of harm will we require before we act? Do we require violence or bodily harm? Do we need to see a legal determination of illegality? What if the offending activity is caused by our user but happens outside of our service?
- What is the nexus of the harm to our service that matters and how far will we go in seeking it out? How much will we investigate who our users are beyond what we can see on our service? This

type of investigation is common—indeed legally required—particularly in the financial services industry.

- How will we apply our policy in a way that is consistent and neutral? Have we ensured that our policy does not have unequal application to different political, religious, or ethnic viewpoints? Are we conscious of how even a neutral policy may be applied disparately to one group or another?

- Are we keeping good records and data about our decisions? Do we audit them?

- How will we provide transparency about what we have done?

- Will there be a right of appeal?

- How will the policy evolve?

Benevolent stewardship is not only an antidote to the lust for monopoly—it can also help end the focus on disruption.

Silicon Valley has tended to look at incumbent companies as frail old institutions ripe for demolition. Uber didn't want to work with taxi providers—it wanted to put them out of business. But disruption like that causes societal upheaval. People get run out of their jobs or lose businesses they've spent their lives building. Those who then feel harmed or left out turn against technology and science, causing the kind of political and social divide we saw in the Trump presidency. In the long run, aggressive disruption is harmful to society, and when society breaks down, it creates ruinous conditions for business.

There's another reason technology needs to move beyond disruption: the industries now being reinvented through technology are bigger and more complex than in the past. No lone tech company is going to disrupt energy or banking. The only way to truly change such industries will be to find the forward-thinking incumbents and work with them, not against them.

I learned this as I got into founding and investing in companies trying to reinvent healthcare. Silicon Valley had by then pumped out hundreds of healthcare startups. Some made well-designed apps or clever devices, yet a lot of health tech companies never found a way to break through, stymied by the complexities of insurance, hospital systems, regulation, and consumer habits. Some of the new tech even added to the burden on physicians, forcing them to spend time on a computer screen instead of focusing on patients, which made healthcare worse. The healthcare system didn't get disrupted. Most of the apps and devices got stuck out on the fringes, far from most people's healthcare experience. Too many startups were launched by engineers who maybe brought in some healthcare advisors but never really understood the complexity of the system.

I have come to see the power of collaboration instead of disruption by working closely on startups with Jefferson Health, a major health system based in Philadelphia, and its CEO, Stephen Klasko. We have all learned from each other, and I realized that tech companies need to understand and integrate with health systems in order to truly change things. Klasko understood that if he can help a new wave of health tech companies take root, his industry has a chance of transforming before it crumbles under the weight of its bad economics. Klasko worked with some of the health tech companies that General Catalyst funded.

The end result of such collaborations will be that a new generation of health tech companies will finally emerge, reinvent healthcare, and bloom into $100 billion companies in harmony with many of the forward-thinking incumbents in healthcare. That opens the way for all of healthcare to transform in ways that are better for everyone involved—especially for those who matter most, the patients and practitioners.

A similar ethos of collaboration is permeating other complex industries. The US insurance industry is enormous—around 6,000 insurance companies write about $1.5 trillion in premiums a year.[4] No startup is going to completely change the insurance game. Yet startups like Lemonade and Salty are succeeding by offering new ways of buying and administering insurance. Our firm funded a startup called Signal Advisors, which is aimed at bringing financial advisory services into the digital era. But it's specifically working with financial advisors, not broadcasting that the company is trying to displace them. Signal's founder, Patrick Kelly, is a former financial advisor. Most financial advisors have clients who need alternative assets such as annuities and life insurance, and typically refer those clients to a firm that does that. The Signal Advisor platform is intended to give advisors a way to keep all of that business—manage money, sell life insurance, sell annuities, and so on, through one platform.

As companies like Lemonade or Signal scale, they will help their ecosystems grow with them—they will expand the pie for insurance and financial advisor services, not snatch the entire pie from everyone in those businesses.

Finally, I want to come back to Tesla. When the company was founded in 2003, it entered an industry—auto manufacturing—that it most certainly was not going to "disrupt" in the Silicon Valley sense of devastating the incumbents and taking over. It was on a mission to change the auto industry by ridding it of internal combustion engines, but by the early 2010s Tesla's leadership understood that it was not going to do that alone. The company needed an ecosystem. It needed friends and it needed competitors. It wanted to pull in new electric car entrepreneurs and influence incumbent car companies.

So, in 2014, CEO Elon Musk wrote a blog post titled "All Our Patent Are Belong to You."[5] It was one of the most visible acts of benevolent stewardship of the past 20 years. It began: "Yesterday, there was a wall of Tesla patents in the lobby of our Palo Alto headquarters. That is no longer the case. They have been removed, in the spirit of the open source movement, for the advancement of electric vehicle technology." Tesla essentially abandoned its patents, giving its R&D to the ecosystem. "Our true competition is not the small trickle of non-Tesla electric cars being produced, but rather the enormous flood of gasoline cars pouring out of the world's factories every day. We believe that Tesla, other companies making electric cars, and the world would all benefit from a common, rapidly-evolving technology platform."

The result is that Tesla has had more influence sooner than Musk or anyone thought it would. Nearly every automaker offers an electric car, and General Motors made its bold proclamation to offer 30 electric vehicles by 2025 and invest in tripling the nation's charging stations.[6] The world is on a path to eliminating gasoline-powered cars, and it wouldn't be happening without the participation of the incumbents that earlier tech companies would have wanted to crush.

If we want technology to lead us to a better world, disruption, breaking things, and driving for monopoly power will never get us there. We need benevolent stewardship.

CHAPTER 12

POLICY PARTNERSHIPS

Technology moves faster than governments. That was true even 100 years ago, when automobiles entered the mainstream. Invented in the 1890s, the number of cars in the United States exploded in the 1910s from 200,000 to 2.5 million. The machines scared horses and endangered pedestrians, who had never before encountered anything moving down a road at 20 miles per hour. The state of Georgia classified cars as ferocious animals. There were almost no laws regulating cars or traffic. The first traffic light went up in 1914 in Cleveland. As late as 1930, a dozen states had no speed limit and 28 states didn't require drivers to have a license.

Government couldn't keep up back then, when technology developed at a more human pace. Now technology moves at the Moore's law pace of computing and the Metcalfe's law pace of networks, while humans have remained pretty much the same. Our policy makers can't process information any faster than the policy makers of 1910.

So now we're dealing with an enormous and growing policy gap that's dangerous for both society and tech companies.

"A genuine public policy crisis for the new economy has emerged," writes Larry Downes, an author and expert on law and technology.[1] He says startups that outrun laws eventually wind up in a distracting or destabilizing fight with regulators, often spurred by legacy businesses protected by old regulations and laws. Think of the hotel industry fighting Airbnb, or taxi companies spurring cities to shut down Uber.

Tech companies do too little to close this tech policy gap. In fact, in the era of "move fast and break things," they typically preferred to ignore and outrun policy, driving a technology's adoption before policy makers even knew much about it. As happened with automobiles a century ago, by the time governments react to developments like, say, facial recognition, the policy makers have to conform to the technology because it's already widely used. In recent years we've seen this happen over and over. Uber blitz-scaled before city and state governments had any idea about its implications for traffic, gig workers, or passenger safety. Facebook helped divide society and upend US politics while US senators, during congressional hearings, famously showed that they didn't even understand how the company made money. Bitcoin, invented in 2009, on some days is worth nearly $1 trillion, yet it is almost completely unregulated anywhere in the world.

This has to change. Today's companies are developing autonomous cars, life-extension technologies, gene editing, AI-fueled videos that look real, and lab-grown meat, while reinventing critical industries such as healthcare and energy. The threat of runaway technology has never been greater. And that also means that the threat of a backlash and reactionary policies has never been greater.

Responsible innovation companies must address policy in a new way. They must approach policy makers as partners and help them understand what's coming and how to govern it intelligently. Companies must understand that regulation is unavoidable and even in many cases necessary or beneficial, so the best course of action is to proactively help shape it. Good regulation can produce greater certainty and lower risk, resulting in less time figuring out the rules and more time focused on working within them.

You've already read in this book about companies that will or have come up against a tech policy gap and need to close it. One is Ginkgo Bioworks, which is working on methods for programming living cells the way someone might program a computer. It's a radical new technology that has implications the company can't yet envision. It's Ginkgo's duty to society and to itself to educate policy makers and guide policy so that the nascent industry can flourish while preventing harmful uses of the technology. You also read about Lenddo, which invented a way to give financial credit to the unbanked by analyzing social media data. It has had to operate in just a few countries because regulators in major economies don't understand it and so reject the concept, even though it could help millions of people get out of poverty. It's Lenddo's duty to itself and society to make regulators comfortable so the technology can spread more widely.

"We're advocating that more and more early-stage companies get involved in policy and government," says Matt Rogers, founder of Incite.org and a cofounder of Nest. "We're at a pivot point in the country and world, like in the 1930s, resetting a lot of regulatory frameworks. And if you want a voice at the table, educate policy makers. And politicians love concrete things to talk about, like a new energy company making innovative batteries."[2]

Given that tech companies until now have been encouraged to ignore policy, the first step in a transition to proactive policy partnerships is to get founders to *think* about policy and the right role for the company. Here are points founders should consider:

- Truly understand the history of policies in your field. Why are they what they are? Are they ancient or recent? What compromises had to be made to get them passed? What were they trying to fix? Keep in mind that most policies were created with good intentions, and enacted to rein in something that had gotten out of control.
- Think through which policies have become obsolete. Few regulations get constantly updated as society and technology change. Many sit on the books decades after they were enacted to solve some problem at the time. Understand what society and technology were like then versus now, and educate policy makers on that context.
- Build products that honor the intent of existing policies while trying to evolve outdated policies. Rolling out a product that blatantly runs afoul of current laws and regulations will hurt your chances of building constructive policy partnerships. Launch within current frameworks. If you've got something in development that pushes the boundaries of existing

policy, be transparent—show it to policy makers and help them understand it.

- Commit resources—money and time—to bringing along policy makers and policy. This is no longer something to do only once the company gets to a certain size or faces its first policy challenge. Investing in policy has become as important as investing in marketing or work spaces. Ignoring it could put the company in peril. Invest from the start, take a long-term view, and make policy partnerships part of the company's responsible innovation mindset and mechanisms.

One more thing: I'm in favor of companies helping to design *policy*, but I believe they should stay away from *politics*. I realize not everyone shares that belief. We are in an extraordinarily divisive time, and we've seen companies assert themselves politically. That ranges from Salesforce pulling out of Indiana over laws that trampled on gay and transgender rights, and companies pulling out of states that enacted voting rights limitations. But in the long run, I believe it's more productive to focus on making policy right no matter who is in office or what those in office stand for. In fact, sticking to the tangibles of policy is probably even more essential during divisive times. Work with everyone, be helpful, develop partnerships, and guide policy so it benefits both business and society.

Once you make a commitment to forming policy partnerships, how do you carry that out?

I've worked on many policy partnerships in the energy sector over the past decade, mostly through an organization I cofounded called Advanced Energy Economy. (I'm still on the board.) AEE strives to help create policies that lead to the adoption of clean, affordable, and secure energy. AEE's CEO, Nat Kreamer, has a lot of experience with how to put policy partnerships in action.[3] Here are recommendations he and I discussed.

The first decision about policy for a company's leadership is: Do I do nothing, do it myself, or do it in coalition?

Doing nothing does not necessarily mean ignoring policy—you may look around at what's happening in your field and hope that other companies are investing in policy and you'll benefit from whatever they achieve. While that's one possible strategy, it is one that could easily backfire and leave your company out of policy discussions.

Doing it yourself can get expensive and your needs might not seem as legitimate to policy makers, who want to hear from an industry not just a company. If you want to influence legislation and regulation, going it alone is not easy. If you just want to educate policy makers, solo might be fine.

Going to policy makers as a coalition is a big investment up front to create the coalition and get members to agree on policy positions. But it has the biggest potential long-run payoff. You can usually identify adjacent companies that would have a common interest. You might start off as a "working group." As the category builds and policy needs get more weighty, you can morph the working group into an association.

However you approach policy makers, start out by helping them get smart about the state of the art. Policy makers don't want to be the complaint department. Help them get credit for doing something good. Make them the bride, not the wedding planner.

Once you start on policy, you have to stay in it. If you're not sure you can commit, do nothing until you can. However, if you wait for something bad to happen to dive in, it's too late.

Go to policy makers early and help them understand what you want and why, but don't ask for anything. Make it clear that you're there to build *their* credibility. These investments in education will pay off when you need something.

Provide financial support for the politicians you think can help you. If you've gotten great at policy and education, you don't have to donate much. The less you invest in getting policy and education right, the more you'll end up investing in individual politicians—and that can cost a lot of money for little long-term payoff.

Finally, remember that this is a dialogue. Educate . . . but also listen. Understand the policy maker's concerns and needs and the context your product is entering into. Listen well enough and you are likely to find ways to tweak your product to give it a competitive advantage over others who don't understand the policy context.

———

The surest way to create good policy partnerships is to build a responsible innovation company.

Build companies that address major issues such as inequality or climate change, or that have a goal of changing society or individual lives for the better, and a policy maker's door is more likely to swing open for you.

The third part of this book discusses mechanisms for ensuring that innovations remain responsible and don't result in harmful unintended consequences. Do those things and you're more likely to avoid the public backlash, antitrust actions, and congressional hearings that companies like Facebook and Google now face.

When considering the future of policy, the subject of one chapter is particularly relevant: algorithm accountability. Companies will be able to develop an AI to watch the company's product and send a warning if it identifies potentially harmful unintended consequences. As technology moves faster and faster, these watchdog AIs should also become an important part of policy and regulation.

As discussed earlier, old-school regulations—like those written by lawmakers and bureaucrats—are too cumbersome to keep up with technology and too "dumb" to monitor algorithms in a timely way. Software-defined regulation can monitor software-driven industries better than regulations enforced by squads of human regulators. Algorithms can watch emerging technologies for details and patterns humans might never catch. If transportation officials want to make sure Uber doesn't shun certain neighborhoods or bias its service, they could rely on an algorithm to look for such behavior.

The watchdog algorithms can be like open-source software—open to examination by anyone. That way, coders can see if they are monitoring the right things, while the companies keep private proprietary algorithms and data.

There's another benefit, perhaps a huge one, to software-defined regulation. It will also show us a path to a more efficient government. The world's legal logic and regulations can be coded into software, and smart sensors can offer real-time monitoring of everything from air and water quality to traffic flows and queues at a Department of Motor Vehicles. Regulators define the rules, technologists create the software to implement them, and then AI and machine learning help refine iterations of policies going forward. This should lead to much more efficient, effective governments at the local, national, and global levels.

The essential point of this chapter is that companies want to avoid stifling and unbending regulations, like those imposed on electric utilities. At the turn of the past century, regulation brought order to the chaos of competing standards and fly-by-night outfits. But in a short time, regulators dictated a "cost-plus" business model for the industry. For decades this meant the utilities had zero incentive to pursue cleaner, more distributed sources of energy or to invest in any innovation at all.

Bottom line: Regulation fostered mindsets and mechanisms in the energy industry that exacerbated climate change. Which cycles back to one of the reasons we need a new generation of responsible innovation companies: so they can turn around the most disastrous unintended consequence of all time.

EPILOGUE

Questions for Companies

As a venture capitalist, I can play a meaningful part in driving responsible innovation and curtailing the unintended consequences of new technology. All VCs can do this. We can influence the way founders think about their mission and the kinds of companies that get funded. At General Catalyst, when we choose where to invest, we test for responsible innovation. Once we invest, we often get a seat on the board or have the CEO's ear, so we can continue to press for responsible innovation as the company grows.

Reflecting on what's in this book, here are 20 questions founders should ask themselves before looking for that next round of funding. When founders come to our firm, they might get asked some of these:

1. **What systemic change do you aspire to create?** Technology can fix some of society's longstanding problems. While the solutions may be hard, they are also some of the biggest opportunities.

2. **Who is the customer, your true north, that you are innovating for?** The best businesses will be those that help individuals in ways never before possible, whether it's helping lower-income people get ahead or giving chronic disease sufferers a better life. Think through the impact on users, and make sure the

offering is built for them, not for a third party, like advertisers. If you are manipulating users for someone else's benefit, you are not innovating responsibly.

3. **Do you understand all the historical interplay of tech, policy, and finance that has led to the opportunity that draws you?** Consumers who are not affluent get stuck with high fees from banks. Consumers with diabetes have an awful experience. There are reasons those situations exist. You need to understand them and then articulate your mission to address that pain point.

4. **What is the minimum virtuous product for your customer?** Don't release a product until you are reasonably certain it will do no harm. Being minimally viable is no longer enough.

5. **Do you have an empowered workforce that has empathy for all stakeholders?** Since most companies serve a diverse customer base, a diverse workforce can help ensure that the company makes products and serves customers in ways that make sense for all kinds of people. Diversity can also help companies better see potential pitfalls.

6. **Do you have a plan for addressing the disruption your business causes for a subset of the stakeholders, including workforces?** Everyone only has so much time, attention, and money. If someone buys from Amazon, they're not buying from a local retailer. If they use an online doctor, they're not visiting a clinic. If your company is hugely successful and creates

massive losses for people in impacted businesses, what can you do to help address that loss?

7. **If you successfully tackle a big problem, what are the second- and third-order implications?** Think through what might go wrong, and how your company would react.

8. **Are you thinking through the multiplier effects of "adjacent" innovations coming true?** You're not operating in a vacuum. As you roll out your innovation, lots of others in adjacent spaces will also introduce innovations. Keep in mind how those other innovations might interplay with what you're doing.

9. **What are the potential unintended consequences of what you're building?** Game out ways the technology could go awry and harm users, whether it's misuse of the product by users or problems that occur with the technology, such as biases creeping into AI. Know that when an unintended consequence causes personal harm, it can severely damage the company. The last thing you want to do is launch a company intending to solve for inequality and inclusion, and then find that your business model encourages you to make choices that exacerbate societal gaps, or your technology includes biases that work against inequality and inclusion.

10. **Who are all the stakeholders impacted by your product?** Decide what you want to see happen to those stakeholders, and then refer back to it as you scale. What experience do you want for employees and their

families? Do you want investors to benefit in the long term or short term?

11. **Are you solving wealth gaps inside the company?** Companies such as PayPal are proving that paying lower-level employees better and giving them a chance to build wealth pays off in the long run.

12. **How do you define market leadership in your category—beyond market share?** The two typically get conflated, but that's not always right. Tesla has a minuscule slice of the automobile market, but it has massively influenced the entire industry.

13. **Does your business model encourage and sustain responsible innovation, or will it pull you toward bad decisions if you have to chase the money?** Good intentions must be matched by financial and governance mechanisms that reinforce them.

14. **What are your KCIs, or key consequence indicators, to go along with your KPIs (i.e., your impact metrics to go along with your economic metrics)?** Companies always understand their KPIs (key performance indicators). It's just as important to know your KCIs and make them a part of management discussions and investor pitches.

15. **What guiding principles will help you resolve tension between KCIs and KPIs as well as short-term versus long-term goals?** If you wait until those tensions arise, it's too late. You'll end up putting out fires and creating ad hoc policies that may not be in your best interest.

16. **What kind of culture can help you achieve your KCIs and KPIs?** Write down a description of the culture

required to realize your mission while maximizing societal and financial metrics. Make sure all your key leaders can articulate it. Hire to build that culture and intentionally cultivate it.

17. **What is the optimal growth rate for stakeholders, society, and sustainability?** Hyperscaling just to win a market space or impress investors is dangerous. It results in poor decisions, damaging mistakes, and bad hires. It's important to grow responsibly.

18. **Do you have a path to becoming a responsible platform that fosters an innovative ecosystem?** The world doesn't need more companies wielding monopoly power to protect their businesses. Create an ecosystem where everyone involved can prosper and innovate.

19. **Are you developing trust and collaboration with policy makers to innovate in lockstep for an enduring business opportunity?** Big systemic change often runs ahead of policy, and that can lead to major problems. Creating policy partnerships can be crucial to responsible innovation. Intentionally think about which policies have become obsolete and how you can constructively work to change them.

20. **How will you measure and sustain the virtue of your product over time?** The most effective way to get ahead of trouble is to use AI to watch for it. The algorithmic canary can also help you self-regulate to stay compliant with existing policies. Make sure you are measuring the consequences of your innovation on *all* your stakeholders.

And finally, there's one overarching question that influences all the others: What do you see the company doing in 100 years? Starting with an infinite timeline is the best way to get a company to think responsibly about the products it builds, the stakeholders it serves, and the society it operates in.

I want my firm, General Catalyst, to be around in 100 years, acting as a driving force for building technology that helps solve great human problems and assures that such technology is good.

I see this book as the start of a global discussion about how to build responsible innovation companies. There is so much to learn and figure out, from what mechanisms really work to support different mindsets to which KCIs best measure a product's impact and the best ways to build algorithmic canaries. I don't want to leave that ongoing work to chance. So with that in mind, I've cofounded Responsible Innovation Labs (RIL), an independent, nonprofit organization funded primarily by tech investors and leaders.

The goal of RIL is to help the next generation of tech companies start and grow in a way that benefits society and helps avoid unintended negative consequences. There are three pillars to RIL's mission:

- Set standards for the practice of responsible innovation.
- Create best-practice tools and playbooks that can help leadership teams build responsible innovation into the fabric of their companies.

- Continue to research, explore, and publish on the topic of responsible innovation.

We want RIL to grow into a coalition that spans the tech and investor communities in Silicon Valley and everywhere else so that the concept of responsible innovation and the goal of ending unintended consequences becomes mainstream. Together, we can make technology good.

ACKNOWLEDGMENTS

From Hemant: Any project like this requires help and support from a lot of people. I want to thank my collaborator, Kevin Maney. Thank you to all of General Catalyst for nuggets of wisdom, anecdotes, day-to-day support, and everything else you do to throw our collective weight behind responsible innovation. I am especially grateful that the partnership has chosen to embrace responsible innovation as a core thesis for the firm and as a key pillar of our mission. In particular, thanks to Jennifer Zimmerman and Molly Gillis for their hands-on involvement with the book, and to my mentor, Ken Chenault, for his leadership, thinking, and support, and for writing this book's foreword.

At Responsible Innovation Labs, thanks to Jon Zieger and Diede van Lamoen for your input. Thank you to our agent, Jim Levine, for your guidance and wisdom, as well as to Casey Ebro, our editor at McGraw Hill, for believing in this book and guiding us to market.

And thank you to my family—Jess, Bella, Arya, and Ajay.

From Kevin: Thanks, first of all, to Hemant and everyone else at General Catalyst for being such great partners on this project, as they have been on each of our three books. Thanks to my colleagues at Category Design Advisors, particularly Mike Damphousse, for being patient when this took time away from other work. And to my longtime editing collaborator, Bob Roe, for giving this a last, sure-handed lift.

We both want to gratefully thank all the people who agreed to be interviewed, either directly for the book or to help increase our knowledge. Apologies if we missed anyone, but the list includes Nan Ransohoff, Jeff Stewart, Peter Reinhardt, Joshua Goldbard, Shishir Mehrotra, James Peyer, Zach Reitano, Matt Rogers, Nat Kreamer, Jason Kelly, Christina Agapakis, Lauren Dunford, Phil Wickham, Josh Reeves, Katie Stanton, Nicole Diaz, Rachel Carlson, Kevin Caldwell, Toyin Ajayi, Jeff Hawkins, David Benigson, Ben Kamens, Daniel Graf, Brian Schimpf, Nitin Nohria, Sue Wagner, and Penny Pritzker.

NOTES

CHAPTER 1

1. "Unintended Consequences," Rob Norton, The Library of Economics and Liberty. https://www.econlib.org/library/Enc /UnintendedConsequences.html

2. *Unscaled: How AI and a New Generation of Upstarts Are Creating the Economy of the Future*, Hemant Taneja with Kevin Maney, PublicAffairs, 2018.

3. "Facebook, Twitter could face punishing regulation for their role in U.S. Capitol riot, Democrats say," Tony Romm, *Washington Post,* January 8, 2021. https://www.washingtonpost.com /technology/2021/01/08/facebook-twitter-congress-trump -riot/

4. "Antitrust Overhaul Passes Its First Tests. Now, the Hard Parts," Cecilia Kang and David McCabe, *New York Times,* June 25, 2021. https://www.nytimes.com/2021/06/24/technology/antitrust -overhaul-congress.html

5. "We Built Google. This Is Not the Company We Want to Work For," Parul Koul and Chewy Shaw, *New York Times,* January 4, 2021. https://www.nytimes.com/2021/01/04/opinion/google -union.html

6. *Reimagining Capitalism in a World on Fire*, Rebecca Henderson, PublicAffairs, 2020, Kindle location 169.

7. "Research: Actually, Consumers Do Buy Sustainable Products," Tensie Whelan and Randi Kronthal-Sacco, *Harvard Business Review*, June 19, 2019. https://hbr.org/2019/06/research -actually-consumers-do-buy-sustainable-products

8. "The Ethical Consumer—US," Mintel, January 2021. https:// store.mintel.com/report/the-ethical-consumer-us-july-2015

9. *Reimagining Capitalism in a World on Fire*, Henderson, Kindle location 173.

10. "The 'Mean Greens' Are Forcing Exxon to Clean Up Its Act," Thomas Friedman, *New York Times,* June 1, 2021. https://www.nytimes.com/2021/06/01/opinion/exxon-mobil-board.html

11. "Policy paper: Agile Nations Charter," United Kingdom, 2021. https://www.gov.uk/government/publications/agile-nations-charter/agile-nations-charter-accessible-webpage-version

12. Musk has been perhaps less responsible in his social media posts about his company, cryptocurrencies, and other topics.

CHAPTER 2

1. "Open Letter to the Airbnb Community about a 21st Century Company," Airbnb. https://news.airbnb.com/brian-cheskys-open-letter-to-the-airbnb-community-about-building-a-21st-century-company/

2. "An Update on Our Work to Serve All Stakeholders," Airbnb. https://news.airbnb.com/serving-all-stakeholders/

3. Kevin Maney has been working with Corning to help document its strategy of "long-cycle innovation." The information in these paragraphs comes from that research.

4. "Key Corporate Responsibility Metrics," Vertex Pharmaceuticals. https://www.vrtx.com/responsibility/key-corporate-responsibility-metrics/

5. "ESG Impact Is Hard to Measure—But It's Not Impossible," Jennifer Howard-Grenville, *Harvard Business Review*, January 22, 2021. https://hbr.org/2021/01/esg-impact-is-hard-to-measure-but-its-not-impossible?registration=success

6. Jeff Hawkins, interview with Kevin Maney, 2021.

7. "Google AI Team Demands Ousted Black Researcher Be Rehired and Promoted," Bobby Allyn, NPR, December 17, 2020. https://www.npr.org/2020/12/17/947413170/google-ai-team-demands-ousted-black-researcher-be-rehired-and-promoted

8. "G.M. Will Sell Only Zero-Emission Vehicles by 2035," Neal E. Boudette and Coral Davenport, *New York Times*, January 28, 2021.

9. Nitin Nohria, interview with Kevin Maney, 2021.

CHAPTER 3

1. "Robinhood CEO: Becoming an investor is the new American dream, just like home ownership was before," Vlad Tenev, CNBC, January 27, 2021. https://www.cnbc.com/2021/01/27 /robinhood-ceo-becoming-an-investor-is-the-new-american -dream-just-like-home-ownership-was-before.html

2. "How Brokerage App Robinhood Got Millennials to Love The Market," Ainsley Harris, *Fast Company*, August 14, 2017. https://www.fastcompany.com/40437888/how-brokerage-app -robinhood-got-millennials-to-love-the-market

3. "Robinhood CEO: We're helping those left behind by Wall Street, not hedge funds," Vlad Tenev, *USA Today*, January 31, 2021. https://www.usatoday.com/story/opinion/2021/01/31 /gamestop-drama-robinhood-had-play-rules-wall-street -column/4332726001/

4. Ben Kamens, interview with Kevin Maney, 2020.

CHAPTER 4

1. Rachel Carlson, interview with Kevin Maney, 2021.

2. "Exploring the relationship between frequency of Instagram use, exposure to idealized images, and psychological well-being in women," M. Sherlock and D.L. Wagstaff, *Psychology of Popular Media Culture*, 2019. https://doi.org/10.1037 /ppm0000182

3. "How an Algorithm Blocked Kidney Transplants to Black Patients," Tom Simonite, *Wired*, October 26. 2020. https://www .wired.com/story/how-algorithm-blocked-kidney-transplants -black-patients/

CHAPTER 5

1. Venture capitalists like me have played a role in widening that gap by making a relatively small group of founders, investors, and early employees superrich—no doubt something that an hourly worker in Oklahoma resents. I'm hoping that, with approaches outlined in this book, our profession can help spread the wealth better than we have.

2. "Share of Total Net Worth Held by the Bottom 50% (1st to 50th Wealth Percentiles)," FRED Economic Data. https://fred .stlouisfed.org/series/WFRBSB50215

3. "Has Wealth Inequality in America Changed over Time? Here Are Key Statistics," Federal Reserve Bank of St. Louis, 2020. https://www.stlouisfed.org/open-vault/2020/december/has -wealth-inequality-changed-over-time-key-statistics

4. "Only the Rich Could Love This Economic Recovery," Karen Petrou, *New York Times,* July 12, 2021. https://www.nytimes.com /interactive/2021/07/12/opinion/covid-fed-qe-inequality.html

5. "Cityblock Health reaches $1B valuation, raises major funding round to address healthcare inequity," Heather Landi, Fierce Healthcare, December 10, 2020. https://www.fiercehealthcare .com/practices/cityblock-health-reaches-1b-valuation-raises -major-funding-round-to-address-healthcare

6. Toyin Ajayi, interview with Kevin Maney, 2020.

7. "How Bone Marrow and Stem Cells Are Collected," BMT Infonet. https://www.bmtinfonet.org/transplant-article/how -bone-marrow-and-stem-cells-are-collected

8. Kevin Caldwell, interview with Kevin Maney, 2020.

9. "Delivering through diversity," Vivian Hunt, Lareina Yee, Sara Prince, and Sundiatu Dixon-Fyle, McKinsey, January 18, 2018. https://www.mckinsey.com/business-functions/organization /our-insights/delivering-through-diversity

10. "Inclusion & Diversity," Netflix. https://jobs.netflix.com/inclusion

11. "Our Positions,"Amazon.com. https://www.aboutamazon.com /about-us/our-positions

12. "Our workforce data," Amazon.com. https://www.aboutamazon .com/news/workplace/our-workforce-data

13. "Diversity, Equity, and Inclusion," Amazon.com. https:// sustainability.aboutamazon.com/people/employees/diversity -inclusion

14. "Bias, disrespect, and demotions: Black employees say Amazon has a race problem," Jason Del Ray, *Recode*, February 26, 2021. https://www.vox.com/recode/2021/2/26/22297554/amazon -race-black-diversity-inclusion

15. "Documentary shows cost of being unbanked," Hadley Malcolm, *USA Today,* June 9, 2014. https://www.usatoday.com /story/money/personalfinance/2014/06/09/american-express -underbanked-documentary/10233259/

16. "PayPal workers were struggling to make ends meet. CEO Dan Schulman vowed to change that," Shannen Balogh and Marguerite Ward, *Insider,* Dec. 29, 2020. https://www .businessinsider.com/paypal-record-breaking-year-plans -transform-capitalism-2020-12

CHAPTER 6

1. "Biden's Recovery Plan Bets Big on Clean Energy," Lisa Friedman and Jim Tankersley, *New York Times,* July 11, 2021. https:// www.nytimes.com/2021/03/23/climate/biden-infrastructure -stimulus-climate-change.html

2. Climate Action. https://www.climateaction100.org/

3. "The State of Climate Tech 2020," PWC. https://www.pwc.com /gx/en/services/sustainability/assets/pwc-the-state-of-climate -tech-2020.pdf

4. Investing in climate tech has been important to me for more than a decade. My investments in climate tech companies are part of what drove me to cofound Advanced Energy Economy.

5. "The State of Climate Tech 2020," PWC. https://www.pwc.com /gx/en/services/sustainability/assets/pwc-the-state-of-climate -tech-2020.pdf

6. "Master Plan, Part Deux," Elon Musk, Tesla, July 20, 2016. https://www.tesla.com/blog/master-plan-part-deux

7. "Bill Gates Says Bitcoin Is Bad for the Planet. He's Not Wrong," Caroline Delbert, *Popular Mechanics,* March 4, 2021. https:// www.popularmechanics.com/science/a35717144/bill-gates -bitcoin-energy-climate/

8. Lauren Dunford, interview with Kevin Maney, 2021.

9. "World population projected to reach 9.8 billion in 2050, and 11.2 billion in 2100," United Nations, June 2017. https:// www.un.org/development/desa/en/news/population/world -population-prospects-2017.html

10. "AeroFarms raises $100m as investors rush to indoor farms," Lindsay Fortado and Emiko Terazono, *Financial Times,* July 8 2019. https://www.ft.com/content/cac48190-9d8a-11e9-9c06 -a4640c9feebb

11. "Bowery Farming is growing crops in warehouses to create food like customized kale," Lora Kolodny and Magdelena Petrova, CNBC, May 24, 2018. https://www.cnbc.com/2018 /05/24/bowery-farming-growing-crops-in-warehouses.html, and "How This Vegetable-Growing Startup Became 400 Times More Productive Than Traditional Farms," Kevin J. Ryan, *Inc.*, (no date). https://www.inc.com/magazine/201806/kevin-j-ryan /aerofarms-vertical-farming.html

12. Peter was my student at MIT in Founders Journey, a course I founded. I invested in Segment when he started it.

13. Peter Reinhardt, interview with Kevin Maney, 2021.

14. Nan Ransohoff, interview with Kevin Maney, 2021.

CHAPTER 7

1. "E-scooters suddenly appeared everywhere, but now they're riding into serious trouble," Julia Buckley, CNN, November 22, 2019. https://www.cnn.com/travel/article/electric-scooter -bans-world/index.html

2. "Hinge's founder gets vulnerable about data, addiction, and 'Modern Love,'" Talib Visram, *Fast Company*, October 24, 2019. https://www.fastcompany.com/90419971/hinges-founder-gets -vulnerable-about-data-addiction-and-modern-love

3. "Exclusive: Hinge is on track to triple its revenue this year, Tinder parent says," Emily Barry, *MarketWatch,* September 22, 2020. https://www.marketwatch.com/story/the-future-of- match-could-hinge-on-an-app-not-named-tinder-11600779714

4. "ESG Impact Is Hard to Measure—But It's Not Impossible," Jennifer Howard-Grenville, *Harvard Business Review*, January 22, 2021. https://hbr.org/2021/01/esg-impact-is-hard-to -measure-but-its-not-impossible

5. Craigslist is a great example of unintended consequences—something that at first seemed harmless and good but then played a major role in destroying newspapers. Company founder Craig Newmark is doing what I hope to avoid: he set up a foundation to fund journalism and newspapers, trying to make up for the consequences he caused.

6. "Collingridge dilemma,"Wikipedia. https://en.wikipedia.org/wiki/Collingridge_dilemma

7. "About the PRI," Principles for Responsible Investment. https://www.unpri.org/pri/about-the-pri

CHAPTER 8

1. "2020 in Review: 10 AI Failures," Synced, January 1, 2021. https://syncedreview.com/2021/01/01/2020-in-review-10-ai-failures/

2. "Online translators are sexist—here's how we gave them a little gender sensitivity training," Stefanie Ullman and Danielle Saunders, *Conversation,* March 30, 2021. https://theconversation.com/online-translators-are-sexist-heres-how-we-gave-them-a-little-gender-sensitivity-training-157846

3. "Aiming for truth, fairness, and equity in your company's use of AI," Elisa Jillson, US Federal Trade Commission, April 19, 2021. https://www.ftc.gov/news-events/blogs/business-blog/2021/04/aiming-truth-fairness-equity-your-companys-use-ai

4. Algorithmic Accountability Act of 2019. https://www.congress.gov/bill/116th-congress/house-bill/2231

5. "For ethical deployments, companies need to explain and trace AI," Roberto Torres, *CIO Dive,* April 7, 2021. https://www.ciodive.com/news/responsible-AI-maturity-report-boston-consulting-group/597996/

6. David Benigson, interview with Kevin Maney, 2021.

7. Jeff Hawkins, interview with Kevin Maney, 2021.

8. "Nuclear Power in the USA," World Nuclear Association. https://www.world-nuclear.org/information-library/country-profiles/countries-t-z/usa-nuclear-power.aspx

9. "Nuclear Power by Company,"Wikipedia. https://en.wikipedia.org/wiki/Nuclear_power_by_country

10. "IEEE Announces Standards Project Addressing Algorithmic Bias Considerations," IEEE. https://standards.ieee.org/news /2017/ieee_p7003.html

CHAPTER 9

1. "HR Startup Zenefits Raises $500 Million at $4.5 Billion Valuation," *Forbes*, May 6, 2015. https://www.forbes.com/sites /briansolomon/2015/05/06/hr-startup-zenefits-raises-500 -million-at-4-5-billion-valuation/?sh=5bf6b1b27dfa
2. Ibid.
3. "The Comeback of a Fallen Tech Unicorn CEO," Amy Feldman, *Forbes*. https://www.forbes.com/sites/amyfeldman /2020/05/28/the-comeback-of-a-fallen-tech-unicorn-ceo/?sh= 52954c7d100a
4. Joshua Reeves, interviews with Kevin Maney, 2020 and 2021.
5. "How Zenefits recovered from scandal in insurance business," Sophia Kunthara, *San Francisco Chronicle*, February 11, 2019. https://www.sfchronicle.com/business/article/How-Zenefits -recovered-from-scandal-in-insurance-13602991.php
6. I was a very early investor in Stripe and watched all this play out.

CHAPTER 10

1. Zach Reitano, interview with Kevin Maney, 2021.
2. Jason Kelly, interview with Kevin Maney, 2021.
3. Christina Agapakis, interview with Kevin Maney, 2021.

CHAPTER 11

1. "Investigation of Competition in Digital Markets." https:// judiciary.house.gov/uploadedfiles/competition_in_digital _markets.pdf
2. "American Entrepreneurship Is Actually Vanishing," *Inc.*, May 2015. https://www.inc.com/magazine/201505/leigh-buchanan /the-vanishing-startups-in-decline.html
3. "Ohio sues Google, seeks to declare the internet company a public utility," Jackie Borchardt, *Columbus Dispatch*, June 8,

2021. https://www.dispatch.com/story/news/politics/2021/06
/08/ohio-sues-google-seeks-declare-search-engine-public
-utility/7602213002/

4. "Insurance Industry at a Glance," Insurance Information
Institute. https://www.iii.org/publications/a-firm-foundation
-how-insurance-supports-the-economy/introduction
/insurance-industry-at-a-glance

5. "All Our Patent Are Belong to You," Elon Musk, Tesla, June 12,
2014. https://www.tesla.com/blog/all-our-patent-are-belong
-you

6. "Electrification," GM.com. https://www.gm.com/commitments
/electrification.html

CHAPTER 12

1. "The top 7 innovations at risk from overzealous regulation,"
Larry Downes, *Washington Post*, October 5, 2015. https://www
.washingtonpost.com/news/innovations/wp/2015/10/05/the
-top-7-innovations-at-risk-from-overzealous-regulation/

2. Matt Rogers, interview with Kevin Maney, 2021.

3. Nat Kreamer, interview with Kevin Maney, 2021.

INDEX

Access to markets, controlling, 132

Advanced Energy Economy, 78, 150

Advertising:
  business model based on, 26–27
  revenue from, 58

Advisory boards, independent, 95

AeroFarms, 80–81

Agapakis, Christina, 125

Agent Orange, 125

Agile Nations Charter, 16

Aging, process of, 43–44

AI:
  accountability for, 105–106
  algorithmic canaries for, 106–109
  biases of, 10, 32–33, 57–58, 103–106
  capabilities of, 106–107
  and company diversity, 32–33
  damage from, 4
  and human longevity, 10
  and job loss, 10
  and language translation bias, 104–105
  master's degree in sustainable, 16
  regulation for, 109–111
  unintended consequences of, 103–106
  weaponry and, 10–11
  (See also Algorithms)

AI growth, 103–111
  algorithmic canaries for, 106–109

government role in, 109–111
  unseen biases in, 103–106

AI-maker generation, 11

Airbnb:
  infinite time horizons at, 23–24, 92, 127
  influencing culture of, 24
  responsible innovation at, 35
  unscaling ability of, 9

Ajayi, Toyin, 63–65

Algorithmic Accountability Act, 105

Algorithmic Bias Considerations, 111

Algorithmic canaries:
  for AI growth, 106–109
  in business models, 96–97
  definition of, 106
  governnments' deployment of, 137
  in product development, 109–110

Algorithms:
  accountability of, 152
  biases of, 57–58
  platform element of, 136–137

Alignment:
  of business and societal interests, x
  capitalism with societal change, 19
  of culture with responsible innovation, 126–127
  of incentives with intentions, 22

"All Our Patent Are Belong To You" (Musk), 143

Allen Institute, 106

Alphabet, 13–14, 27, 80
Alphabet Workers Union, 13–14
Alzheimer's, 43
Amazon:
    and AWS, 46–47, 118, 138
    concentration of power and,
        11
    diversity at, 69–70
    and platform responsibility,
        136–137
    problems solved by, 92–93
    retail transformed by, 98–99
    as technology monopoly,
        131–133
    unintended consequences
        of, 6
Amazon Web Services (AWS),
    118, 138
American Airlines, 77
American Express, ix, xi, 24, 70
American Express Ventures, ix
"An Open Letter to the Airbnb
    Community About
    Building a 21st Century
    Company," 23
Android, 135
Antiaging, unintended
    consequences of, 44–45
Antitrust law, 131–138
    failure of, 133
    to protect business
        ecosystems, 11
    violations of, 131
AOL, 131
API (application programming
    interface), 119
Apple, 11, 46, 76, 131, 132–133
Application programming
    interface (API), 119
Apps, addictive, 41
Artificial intelligence (see AI)
Atomic energy, 109–110
Atomic Energy Act, 109
Atomic Energy Commission,
    109

AT&T, 131
Automobiles:
    and climate change, 6
    electric vehicles, 143–144
    invention of, 145
Autonomous Research, 41
AWS (Amazon Web Services),
    118, 138

Bank of America, 77
Barra, Mary, 33
Basic infrastructure, 139
Battery technology, 17
Benevolent stewardship, 131,
    138, 140
Benigson, David, 107
Bezos, Jeff, 80
Bhatt, Baiju, 40
Bias(es):
    in AI, 10, 103–106
    against Black patients, 57–58
    removing AI, 32–33
    in search results, 13
Biden, Joseph, 75
Big tech (see Technology
    monopolies)
Bing, 135
Bioengineering, 124
Bio-oil sequestration, 81
Bird (company), 87
Bitcoin, 77, 146
Black people:
    and facial recognition
        technology, 10
    family wealth disparities for,
        61–62
    healthcare bias against, 57–58
Black@Netflix, 69
Blecharczyk, Nathan, 23
Blitzscaling (Hoffman), 97
Blockchain, 47
Blumenthal, Richard, 12
Board, choosing, 120
Boston, 57
Boston Consulting Group, 106

Bowery Farming, 80–81
Branding, 94
BrightFarms, 80
Brokerage commissions,
 reliance on, 114
Brookings Institution, 107, 135
Business alignment, x
Business creation, falling, 135
Business ecosystems, 11, 98,
 100, 142
Business model(s), 87–101
 algorithmic canaries in,
  96–97
 analysis of unintended
  consequences in, 93–94
 and company culture, 94–95
 and corporate governance, 95
 of disengagement, 92–93
 of e-scooter companies,
  87–88
 for ethical growth, 97
 of Facebook, 89
 faulty, 27
 of Hinge, 90
 infinite time horizons for, 92
 with KCIs, 95–96
 of manipulation, 56–57
 matching mindset and
  mechanism in, 91–101
 modeling future scenarios
  for, 99–100
 for partnerships with
  regulators, 98–99
 performance of, 116
 responsible innovation baked
  in, xii
 for stakeholder capitalism,
  97–98
 venture capitalists' role in,
  100–101
Business purpose, 63–67
Business Roundtable, 15

Caldwell, Kevin, 66–67
Caley Thistle, 103

California, 114
Cambridge Judge Business
 School, 28
Cambridge University, 16
Capitalism:
 environmental stewardship
  and, 78
 for good, 91
 positive change from, 19
 right kind of, 83
Carbon footprint, of factories,
 79–80 (*See also* Climate
 change)
Carbon removal, 81–82
Carlson, Rachel, 51
Cave, Stephen, 16
Charm Industrial, 81–82
Checks and balances:
 governance for, 129
 on growth, 115–116
Chenault, Ken, 24
Chesky, Brian, 23–24, 92
Chipotle, 52
Chrysler, 34
Cityblock:
 healthcare for marginalized
  communities and, 18,
  32, 55
 mechanism at, 91
 responsibility at, 35
 responsible innovation at,
  63–65
 unscaling ability of, 9
Clayton Act, 133
Climate Action 100+ initiative,
 75
Climate change, 73–83
 AeroFarms address of, 80–81
 and bitcoin, 77
 Bowery Farming address of,
  80–81
 Charm Industrial address of,
  81–82
 Guidewheel address of, 75–77
 innovation at Tesla, 16–17

Climate change (*continued*)
opportunity in addressing, 33
responsible innovation
companies for, 153
Stripe Climate address of,
82–83
and twentieth-century
technology, 73–74
Climate-related companies, 75
Clinton Corn Processing
Company, 6
Clubhouse session, 77
CNBC.com, 40
Coalitions, policy decisions in,
150
Collaboration, company
creation with, xi
College-education, advantage
of, 61–62
Collingridge, David, 99
Collingridge Dilemma, 99–100
Colorado, 51
Commission-free trading, 40
Community colleges, 51–52
Companies:
creation of, xi
enduring, ix
leadership of, and policy
partnerships, 150–151
obligation of, xii
protection for smaller, 136
social purpose of, 14–15
values of, 122–123
Company responsibility, 94
"Connected pregnancy care,"
55
Connecticut, 12
Conrad, Parker, 113–114
Consumer-facing website, 139
Conway, Jill Ker, 96
Corning, 24–26, 35, 127
Corningware, 25
Corporate governance, 95
Corporate social responsibility,
5

Council for Inclusive
Capitalism, 16
COVID-19 pandemic, xi, 4, 7–8,
62, 70
Craigslist, 98
CRISPR, 47
Culture, 121–129
at Airbnb, 24
creating diverse and
inclusive, 68
defining, 121
at Ginkgo Bioworks, 124–126
instilling, 94
intentionality of, 126–128
responsible innovation in, xii
at Ro, 121–124
that weighs short-term
tactics and long-term
goals, 127
Curiosity, as company value,
122–123
Customer experience, 115
Customers, platform element
of, 136–137

Data, platform element of,
136–137
Deep fakes, 10, 90
Deloitte, 68
Deming, Edwards W., 34–35
Department of Motor Vehicles,
153
Diabetes, 18, 29–30, 54–55
Dialogue, with policy makers,
151
Disengagement, 18, 90
business models of, 92–93
striving for, 29–30
Disney, 52
Disruption:
and stewardship, 140–141
technology for, xi
from unscaling, 9
Diversity:
and AI, 32–33

company's address of, xiii
initiative to address
inequality, 67–71
Divestment, 136
Doctoroff, Dan, 63
Dow Jones industrial average,
15
Downes, Larry, 146
Dream@Netflix, 69
Drones, weapon-carrying, 90
Dunford, Jason, 78–79
Dunford, Lauren, 78–80

Economic gap (*see* Wealth gaps)
Economic opportunity, xii–xiii
"Economies of Unscale"
(Taneja), x
Economy, equitable, 56
Ecosystems, business, 11, 98,
100, 142
ED (erectile dysfunction), 122
Edison, Thomas, 25
Education benefits, 51–52
Effective, as company value,
122–123
Efficiency, of farming and
manufacturing, 76
Electric system, sustainable,
76–77
Electric vehicles, 143–144 (*See
also* Tesla)
Elizabeth, Queen, 10
Empathic entrepreneur,
118–119
Empathy:
as central to culture, 122
as company value, 122–123
at scale, 50
Employee experience, for
checks and balances on
growth, 115–116
Employee ownership, 125
"Employee relief fund," 70
Employee Resource Groups, at
Netflix, 69

Employers, education benefits
from, 51–52
Endurance, 13, 22
building companies for, 97
culture of, 127
innovation and, 58–59
planning for, 26–27
(*See also* Infinite time
horizons)
Energy General Fusion, 76
Enforcement, of antitrust law,
131–138
Engagement:
goal of, 29
and manipulation, 58
model of, 41
Entangled Group, 53
Entrepreneurs, empathic,
118–119
Entrepreneurship, erosion of,
133–134
Environmental stewardship, 78
Environmental sustainability,
xiii
"The Era of 'Move Fast and Break
Things' Is Over" (Taneja), xi
Erectile dysfunction (ED), 122
Error, as unintended
consequence, 7
E-scooter companies, 87–89
ESG metrics (environmental,
social and governance),
28–29, 75, 95–96, 101
Ethical growth, 113–120
business models for, 97
at Gusto, 115–118
irresponsible tactics and, 118
responsible scaling for,
119–120
at Zenefits, 113–116
(*See also* Responsible
innovation)
European Union, 135–136
and AI accountability, 105
regulators, 12

Everlane, 33
"Explainable AI," 107–108
External impact measurement, 28
ExxonMobil, 15

Facebook:
  advertising on, 51
  algorithms used on, 106
  business models of, 89
  concentration of power and, 11
  financial incentives and behavior of, 26–27
  and Instagram, 56
  irresponsible behavior by, 12, 93
  morale at, 13–14
  regulation of, 110
  as technology monopoly, 131–133, 136
  and technology policy, 146, 152
  unintended consequences of, 6
  in winner-take-all economy, 117
Facial recognition technology, 10, 89
Factories, carbon footprint of, 79–80
Fake news, 27
Farming:
  improving efficiency of, 76
  indoor data-driven, 80–81
Fast Company, 41, 90
FDA (Food and Drug Administration), 98–99
Federal Artificial Intelligence Agency, 109
Federal Reserve Bank of St. Louis, 61
Fiber optics, 25
Financial guidance, for low-income people, 55–56

Financial incentives, for unethical behavior, 27
Financial industry, 54–55
Financial Industry Regulatory Authority, 13
Financial inequality, addressing, 71
Financial returns, 3
Financial stress, of pandemic, 70
Fink, Larry, 14
Fintech Strategy, 41
"First mover advantage," as myth, 118
Food and Drug Administration (FDA), 98–99
Forbes, 113
Ford, 34
Ford, Henry, 73–74, 77
Forethought, company creation with, xi
Fortune 500 companies, 17
Francis, Pope, 16
Friedman, Milton, 5, 19, 62, 133
Friedman, Thomas, 15
Fulcher, Jay, 116
Future scenarios, for business models, 99–100

GameStop, 41–42
Gates, Bill, 77
Gebbia, Joe, 23
Gebru, Timnit, 33
Gene-editing technology, 90
General Catalyst:
  Kenneth Chenault at, ix, 24
  impact investing by, 12, 18, 142
  unscaling at, 9
  as venture capital firm, x, xiii
General Motors, 17, 33
Genomics, 47
Ginkgo Bioworks, 124–126, 147
Glassdoor, 116
GM, 35

Gmail, 135
Google:
  advertising on, 51
  and AI, 104
  concentration of power and,
    11
  employee dissatisfaction at,
    13–14
  and first-mover advantage,
    118
  irresponsible behavior at,
    26–27
  irresponsible behavior of, 12
  lack of diversity at, 33
  as platform, 136
  as public utility, 135
  as technology monopoly,
    131–133
  and technology policy, 152
  in winner-take-all economy,
    117
Governance:
  corporate, 95
  defining, 121
  ESG metrics (*see* ESG metrics)
  factors to consider for, 121
  platform, 136–140
Government's role:
  in AI growth, 109–111
  in deployment of algorithmic
    canaries, 137
  in regulation of monopolies,
    135–136
Green New Deal, 75
Greenwashing, 5, 77
Grover (algorithm), 106–107
Grow, 125–126
Guidewheel, 75–77, 91
Guild Education:
  business model of, 58, 91
  creation of, 51–53
  culture of endurance at, 127
  unscaling ability of, 9
Gusto:
  culture of endurance at, 119

ethical growth at, 115–118
responsible innovation at, 18,
  117–118
unscaling ability of, 9

Hacker-entrepreneur, 118
Hard innovation, investment
  in, 26
Harm, magnitude of, 139
Harvard Business Review, x
Harvard Business School, 14, 35
Harvard University, 14
Hawkins, Jeff, 30, 108
Healthcare, 18
  evolution of, x
  and individual impact, 54–55
  marginalized patients and,
    63
  startups, 141
  systemic change in, 31
  transformation of, 142
  (*See also* Cityblock; Ossium;
    Ro)
Henderson, Rebecca, 14
Higher-level application, 139
High-fructose corn syrup, 6
Hinge, business models of, 90
Hoffman, Reid, 97
Honda, 34
Houghton, Jamie, 25
Howard-Grenville, Jennifer,
  28–29, 96
Human longevity, AI and, 10
Hypergrowth:
  irresponsibility of, 117–120
  risk factor of, 100
Hyperscale, drive for, 21

IBM, 6, 8, 11, 131
IEEE (Institute of Electrical and
  Electronics Engineers), 111
Ignorance, as unintended
  consequence, 7
Imperious immediacy of
  interest, 7

Impersonal nature, of
scaled-up economy, 53
Impossible Foods, 33, 76
Incite.org, 147
Inclusion:
Amazon practices and, 69–70
building products that help
with, 32
company practices of, 32–33
company's address of, xiii
initiatives to address
inequality, 67–71
Indiana, 149
Individual consumers,
products tailored for, 8–9
Individual impact, 31–32, 49–59
and AI infused biases, 57–58
financial industry for, 54–55
at Guild Education, 51–53
healthcare for, 54–55
at Instagram, 54–55
negative, 57
positive, 58–59
of unscaled technologies,
49–50
Individualized fitness, 55
Indoor farming, 80–81
Industries, reinventions of,
117–118
Inequality, 61–71
AI to look for consequences
of, 108
building products that solve,
32
businesses designed to
address, 63–67
company practices of
inclusion and, 32–33
diversity and inclusion
initiative to address, 67–71
societal issue of, 61–62
unintended consequences
and, 104
Infinite time horizons:
at Airbnb, 23–24

board members belief in, 128
for business models, 92
"Innocent monopolies," 133
Innovation, endurance and,
58–59
"Innovation for good," xii
Innovation protection, 137
Inputs measurement, 96
Insider, 71
Instagram, 41, 54–55, 57
Institute of Electrical and
Electronics Engineers
(IEEE), 111
Insurance, 56
Intentionality:
company creation with, xi
of culture, 126–128
relying on, 30–31
Intentions:
alignment of incentives with,
22
metrics for success in
meeting, 24
Investigation of users, 140
Investment, reasons for, 3, 12
Investors, choosing, 120
iPhone, 46, 131, 136
Irresponsibility:
in growth, 115
in innovation, 118
in tactics, 118
in technology, 12–16
Israel, 55, 103
Italy, 16

Japan, 16
Japanese companies, 34–35
Jefferson Health, 141
Jeopardy! (television show), 47
Jillison, Elisa, 105
Job loss, AI and, 10

Kahn, Mark, 127
Kamens, Ben, 44–46
Kauffman Foundation, 135

Kelly, Jason, 124–126
Kelly, Patrick, 142
Key consequence indicators
    (KCIs), 22, 95–96, 109
Key performance indicators
    (KPIs), 27–28
Khan Academy, 9
Klasko, Stephen, x, 141–142
Koul, Parul, 13
KPIs (key performance
    indicators), 27–28
Kreamer, Nat, 78, 150

Language translation bias,
    104–105
Leadership standards, xii
Legislative requirements, 136
Lemonade (company), 56, 142
Lenddo, 56, 147
Life expectancy, extending, 44–45
Lime (company), 87
LinkedIn, 97, 117
Livongo Health:
    business model of, 58
    and disengagement, 29–30,
        54–55
    and healthcare system, 19
    impact on individuals by, 31
    responsible innovation at, 18
    scale of, 119
    unscaling ability of, 9
London, 101, 118
Long time horizons, 115
Long-term goals, 127
Los Angeles Unified School
    District, 53
Low-income people:
    financial guidance for, 55–56
    in United States, 51

Magic, as company value,
    122–123
Manipulation:
    business model of, 56–57
    of engagement, 58

Manufacturing, efficiency
    of, 76
Marginalized communities,
    healthcare in, 18
Marginalized groups, harm of
    AI on, 33
Marginalized patients, 63
Market dominance, of tech
    companies, 133–134
Markets:
    defining, 133–134
    mass vs. niche, 47
Mass markets, 47
Massachusetts Institute of
    Technology (MIT), 124
"Master Plan, Part Deux"
    (Musk), 76–77
McKinsey, 68
McLeod, Justin, 90
McNamee, Roger, 11
Measurement:
    of improving society, 95–96
    of the right things, 27–29
Mechanism:
    in business models, 91–101
    for responsible innovation
        companies, 22–23
    to support mindset, 65, 67,
        77, 115
Medical technologies, 9
Merck, 17
Merton, Robert, 7
Metcalfe's law, 3–4, 145
Metrics:
    to focus on what a company
        is doing, 28
    on how a company is doing,
        28
    for success in meeting
        intentions, 24
    (See also specific metrics)
Micromobility, sector of, 76
Microsoft, 11, 76, 131
Mindset:
    in business models, 91–101

Mindset (*continued*)
  mechanism to support, 65,
    67, 77, 115
  for responsible innovation
    companies, 22–23
Mindstrong, 35
Minimum viable products, 21,
  30
Minimum virtuous products,
  21, 30–31
Mintel, 14
Misinformation campaigns, 108
MIT (Massachusetts Institute of
  Technology), 124
Model T, 73–74
Monopolies:
  government regulation of,
    135–136
  technology, 11
Moore's law, 3–4, 145
Moral resource, culture as,
  127–128
Morale, at Facebook, 14
Musk, Elon, 17, 39, 76–77,
  143–144

Nadler, Jerrold, 12–13
National economy, 135
Nazi Germany, 6
Nest, 147
Netflix, 58, 68–69, 118
Net-zero carbon emissions, 75
New Jersey, 10, 80
New York City, 40, 80, 118
New York State, 12, 75
New York Times, 12–15, 75
Next-generation companies, x
Niche markets, 47
Nike, 96
Nohria, Nitin, 35
Noodle.ai, 107
Nothing, as policy decision, 150
Nuclear Regulatory
  Commission (NRC), 109
Numenta, 30, 108

Nuvo, 55
NYU Stern Center for
  Sustainable Business, 14

Obligation, of companies, xii
Ocasio-Cortez, Alexandria, 75
Occupy Wall Street movement,
  40
Ohio, 135
1 percent, 61–62
Open source movement, 143
Opportunity gaps, 61–62
Optimal growth rate, 119
Organ donation, 66–67
Outcomes, 96
Oxford Photovoltaics, 76
OxyContin, 6

Palm Pilot, 30, 108
Palo Alto, 143
Parks, Nijeer, 10
Partnerships, with regulators,
  98–99
Personal problems, technology
  to solve, 49
Philadelphia, 141
Pichai, Sundar, 27, 33
Pixellot, 103
Planet Labs, 76
Platform governance, 136–140
Platform misuse, 139
Platform responsibility,
  136–137
Policy(-ies):
  algorithm accountability for,
    152
  context of, 148
  development of, 138–140
  evolving, 140
  history of, 148
  honoring existing, 148–149
  making decisions about, 150
  neutrality of, 140
Policy makers:
  building credibility of, 151

responsible innovation
companies partnering
with, 147
Policy partnerships, 145–153
company leadership and,
150–151
regulation and, 147–149
software-defined regulation
for, 152–153
technology policy gap and,
145–146
transitioning to proactive,
148–149
Political videos, 27
Politics, staying out of, 149
Polman, Paul, 17–18
Positive change, from
capitalism, 19
Positive impact, investment
for, 3
The Predictive Index, 32
Principles for Responsible
Investment (PRI), 101
Privacy:
of customers, xiii
invasions of, 27, 108
Proactive policy partnerships,
148–149
Product development, 109–110
Profit:
ignoring unintended
consequences for, 7
from socially responsible
businesses, 19–20
Protection, for smaller
companies, 136
Public, as guinea pigs, 30
Public utility, Google as, 135
Purpose:
business, 63–67
social, 14–15
PWC report, 75
Pyrex, 25

Quality movement, 33–34

Racial discrimination, 108
Radical collaboration, 127
Radical empathy, 50, 58
Ransohoff, Nan, 82–83
R&D investment, 26
Records, auditing, 140
Reddit, 42, 104
Reeves, Joshua, 113, 115–116
Regulation:
algorithm accountability for,
152
and policy partnerships,
147–149
*Reimagining Capitalism in a
World on Fire* (Henderson),
14
Reinhardt, Peter, 81
Reitano, Zach, 121–124
Relentlessness, as company
value, 122–123
Resources, commitment of, 149
Responsibility:
companies showing, 14
in decision making, 123–124
in growth, 117–120
for technology, 5–6
in technology, 47
Responsible innovation:
agenda for, 128
best returns from, 5
board members belief in, 128
companies with, 22–23, 147,
153
culture alignment with,
126–127
at General Motors, 33
for technology products, 4–5
Responsible innovation thesis,
xi
Responsible scaling, 119–120
Return plus impact, seeking,
31–35
Revenue, from advertising, 58
Revolution Foods, 78
Rhamanian, Saman, 121

Right to appeal, 140
Right-scaled companies,
    119–120
Ro, 9, 121–124
Robinhood Financial:
    fines for, 13
    and suicide, 49
    systemic change at, 40–43
    unintended consequences at,
        50, 59
Rogers, Matt, 147–148
Roman (company), 121
Romer, Roy, 51
Romm, Iyah, 63
Rosenberg, David, 81

Safi (*see* Guidewheel)
Salesforce.com, 138, 149
Salty, 142
San Diego, 87
San Francisco, 80, 87
San Francisco Chronicle, 116
Santa Monica, 87
Scale:
    economies of, 8, 53
    responsibility in, 119–120
    for students, 52–53
Schmidt, Eric, 80
Schulman, Dan, 70–71
Schutz, Rob, 121
Scoot, 87
Scotland, 103
Scottish Inverness Caledonian
    Thistle FC, 103
Seattle, 87
Securities and Exchange
    Commission, 114
Shaw, Chewy, 13
Sherman Act, 133
Short-term tactics, 127
Sidewalk Labs (Google), 63
Signal Advisors, 142
Signal AI, 107
"Silicon Valley Dreams"
    (Taneja), xi

Singapore, 16, 56, 87
Six Sigma Manufacturing, 35
Smaller companies, protection
    for, 136
Snap, 134
The Social Control of Technology
    (Collingridge), 99
Social isolation, 108
Social purpose, 14–15
Social Security Administration,
    6
Socially responsible businesses,
    19–20
Societal change:
    capitalism alignment with, 19
    and emerging technologies,
        46–47
    and inequality, 61–62
    measurement of, 95–96
Societal interests, alignment
    with, x
SoftBank, 80
Software-defined regulation,
    152–153
Software-driven industries, 110
Sokolin, Lex, 41
Solar energy industry, 17
Solar Roof, 17
Spent (Schulman), 70
Spring Discovery:
    longevity at, 18
    systemic change at, 44–46
Sprinklr, 107
Stakeholder capitalism, 97–98
Stakeholders:
    benefits for all, 26
    serving all, 24
Stanford University, 16, 51,
    78–79
Startups, 117–118
Stem cell treatments, 65–67
Stewardship, 131, 138–144
    benevolent, 131, 138, 140
    collaboration and, 141–142
    disruption and, 140–141

platform governance for, 138–140
at Tesla, 143–144
Steyer, Tom, 78
Stitch Fix, 31–32
Stock set up, 128
Stripe, 9, 33, 138
Stripe Climate, 82–83
Students, scale for, 52–53
Subscription service, model of, 115
Suicide, 49
Sustainable consumer products, 14
Sustainable energy, 76–77
Systemic change, 31, 39–47
and emerging technologies, 46–47
at Robinhood Financial, 40–43
at Spring Discovery, 44–46

Tailored products, 50
Talent, retaining, 14
Technology(-ies):
battery technology, 17
and climate change, 6
climate change and, 73–74
for disruption, xi
emerging technology, 46–47
as enabler, ix, xiii
ethical deployment of, xiii
facial recognition technology, 10, 89
gene-editing technology, 90
irresponsibility in, 12–16
medical technologies, 9
positive aspects of, 7–8
responsibility for, 5–6, 47
responsible innovation for, 4–5
to solve personal problems, 49
threat of runaway, 146
unintended consequences of, x
unscaled, 50, 54

Technology monopolies:
and antitrust law, 131–138
bills reforming, 12–13
concerns about, 11
dangers of, 134–135
legislative requirements for, 136–137
national economy and, 135
Technology policy gap, 145–146
Technology sector:
disruption vs. innovation in, 140–141
founders controlling governance in, 128
ideals of, 118, 124
myths from, 97
views of growth by, 115
Teenage girls, 57
Teledoc, 18, 55, 118
Tenev, Vlad, 40, 43
Tesla:
climate change innovation at, 16–17, 19, 39, 76–77
and market domination, 118
problem solved by, 93
stewardship at, 143–144
Threat, of runaway technology, 146
3D printing, 47
Top 1 percent, 61–62
Total Quality Management, 35
Toyota, 34
Trading, commission-free, 40
Traditional healthcare, 54
Trainiac, 55
Transformation, 39–40
Trump, Donald, 12, 140
Tullman, Glen, 18
Twilio, 127
Twitter, 7, 117

Uber, 118, 126, 146
Underlying conditions, 64
Unethical behavior, incentives for, 27

UnHealthcare (Klasko, Teneja, Maney), x–xi
Unilever, 17–18
Unintended consequence(s):
  of AI, 103–106
  AI to anticipate, 108–109
  of Amazon, 6
  of antiaging, 44–45
  in business models, 93–94
  culture as defense against, 124–125
  of e-scooters, 87–89
  of Facebook, 6
  foreseeing, 18
  ignorance and error as, 7
  imperious immediacy of interest as, 7
  and inequality, 104
  of medical technologies, 9
  of technology, x
  transformation and, 39–40
  of Twitter, 7
  of YouTube, 6–7
Union organization, at Alphabet, 13–14
United Arab Emirates, 16
United Kingdom, 16
United Nations, 101
U.S. Capitol, storming of, 12
U.S. Congress, 12, 105, 110, 132
U.S. Department of Justice, 134
U.S. Federal Trade Commission, 105
U.S. insurance industry, 142
U.S. Securities and Exchange Commission, 13
U.S. Senators, 146
University of Cambridge, 96
University of Phoenix, 51
Unscaled (Taneja and Maney), x–xi, 8
Unscaled economies, 8–9, 50–53
Unscaled technologies, 49–50

Unscaling, 8–9
Upskill, 51
Upward Farms, 80
USA Today, 43

Vatican, 15–16
Venture capitalist investments, 75
Venture capitalists, role of, 100–101
Vertex Pharmaceuticals, 28
Viagra, 122
Virtual reality, 47
VP of Ethical Use, 127

WallStreetBets, 42
Walmart, 52, 53
Washington Post, 12
Watchdog algorithms, 110
Watson (IBM), 47
Wealth gaps, 4, 61–62, 70
Weaponry, 10–11
Weeks, Wendell, 25
Winner-take-all economy, 117
Woodbridge, 10
World War II, 6, 109

Yost, Dave, 135
Yourself, making policy decisions, 150
YouTube:
  AI learning from, 104
  as platform, 138
  problem solved by, 92–93
  unintended consequences of, 6–7

Zenefits:
  changing culture of, 126
  ethical growth at, 113–116
  hyperscaling at, 13
Zoom, 76
Zucked (McNamee), 11
Zuckerberg, Mark, 11, 27, 89

ABOUT THE AUTHORS

Hemant Taneja is a managing director at the venture capital firm General Catalyst and has been featured on the *Forbes* Midas List of top venture investors. He partners with mission-driven founders building platform companies that are fundamentally aligned with the long-term interests of society. He and General Catalyst are early investors in companies including Airbnb, Commure, Gusto, Livongo, Mindstrong, Oscar, Ro Health, Samsara, Snap, Stripe, and Warby Parker. In 2018, Hemant (with Kevin) published *Unscaled*, which outlines his investment thesis of "economies of unscale." In 2020, he, Kevin, and Steve Klasko published *UnHealthcare*, about the impact of AI on health and the emergence of the health assurance category.

Kevin Maney is a bestselling author, technology journalist, and a founding partner of Category Design Advisors. His previous books include *Unscaled*; *Play Bigger: How Pirates, Dreamers, and Innovators Create and Dominate Markets*; and *The Maverick and His Machine: Thomas Watson Sr. and the Making of IBM*. He has written for dozens of media outlets, including *USA Today, Fortune, Wired,* and *Newsweek,* and has appeared regularly on television and radio, including CNN, CNBC, NPR, and *CBS Sunday Morning.*